Please return / renew by date shown.
You can renew it at:
r norlink.norfolk.gov.uk
or by telephone: 0344 800 8006
Please have your library card & PIN ready

M.

NORFOLK LIBRARY
AND INFORMATION SERVICE

D1340503

Larks

Published by the Larks Press

Ordnance Farmhouse, Guist Bottom
Dereham, Norfolk NR20 5PF
01328 829207
Larks.Press@btinternet.com
www.booksatlarkspress.co.uk

Printed by the Lanceni Press
Garrood Drive, Fakenham
01328 851578
April 2006
Reprinted October 2006

Reprinted by Newprint and Design Ltd
In March 2010

Picture credits are on page 208.

British Library Cataloguing-in-Publication Data
A catalogue record for this book is available
from the British Library.

ISBN 1 904006 30 2

This book is dedicated to
the memory of
my mother

Table of Contents

Preface

This book is the result of the many hours of interviews we conducted with Ethel George in 2003-05. Ethel is a vivacious 91-year-old lady with remarkably fresh memories of her childhood in Norwich. She was born in 1914 as the seventeenth and last child of Albert Edwards, a bricklayer, and his wife Eleanor. She grew up near Barrack Street, between Steward and Patteson's vast Pockthorpe Brewery and the old Cavalry Barracks, one of the poorest neighbourhoods in the city. Our interviews took place in Ethel's present home and usually lasted two hours. We fitted a hands-free microphone around her neck, asked her to shut her eyes, imagine herself back in her childhood, and then recount all she 'saw' and remembered. Ethel seemed to be able to transport herself back in time. She conjured up fascinating memories of her past and described them in colourful detail and in an inimitable Norwich idiom. We recorded all she said and the original tapes with our transcriptions are now in the keeping of the Norfolk Sound Archive at the Norfolk Records Centre.

This book covers the first twenty years of Ethel's life, the period of the First World War and its aftermath. This was the last period in which poor people in Norwich lived without electric lighting and could die because they were too poor to buy adequate food or medical care. Ethel lived in a three-bedroom house and her family was better off than many. However, life was still very hard, particularly in view of the large size of the family: each bed had to be shared between four or five siblings; clothes had to be handed down and mended and re-mended, and Ethel's poor mother's ingenuity was stretched to the limit in finding enough food to keep all her children from going hungry.

Ethel helps us to understand what it was like to live in a poor neighbourhood. She talks of how families like hers constantly battled to maintain the symbols of respectability, such as the cloth on the table and the clean clothes on Sunday, so that they would not be confused with the abject poor who lived in the unsanitary and over-crowded courtyards close by. She comments on the large proportion of men's income that was spent on drink and on the fighting and abuse that the alcohol fueled. She remembers the difficult relationships between authority figures and the people of her neighbourhood – the strictness of the school and Sunday School teachers, the harshness of the local officials making decisions on means-tested social benefits, the ankles kicked by policemen administering their summary justice. Despite the difficulties, Ethel remembers a happy childhood. She recalls her friends and the games they played in the streets and out on the wilds of Mousehold Heath. She remembers sitting round the fire and singing songs with her family in those pre-radio days. She remembers the excitement of Christmas and the traditions associated with this and the other holidays. She also remembers the great annual treat of a trip to the seaside in Great Yarmouth when, with picnic and chamber pot packed, the family would take their only train journey of the year.

In the second part of her narrative, Ethel recalls her teenage years. She left school on her fourteenth birthday and began working in the boot and shoe trade. She vividly recalls the noises and the smells of her early working days and the long hours she worked. She remembers how thrilled she was when her parents allowed her to keep back enough money from her pay packet to buy some clothes, get her hair styled and go off with friends to the dances in Chapelfield Gardens. She explains how she met her first husband Dick while promenading with her girl friends up and down the Prince of Wales Road, and how he entered an unregulated boxing competition to win the money to buy her an engagement ring.

It is a rich story and brings back into memory some heroic characters who do not deserve to be forgotten, none more so than Ethel's mother who grew up in a fairly comfortable home with a servant and who could never have dreamed of the long life of toil and privation that lay before her.

In preparing this book, we organized what Ethel told us into separate themes and into chronological order. We did some editing to smooth the joins in the material, but, apart from this, the narrative comes directly from Ethel. Any material that we added to clarify word meanings or to provide historical background material has been set out in footnotes.

Finally, Ethel told us that she would like this book to be a tribute to her mother and to all the other women in her neighbourhood, who succeeded in raising their children in such difficult conditions.

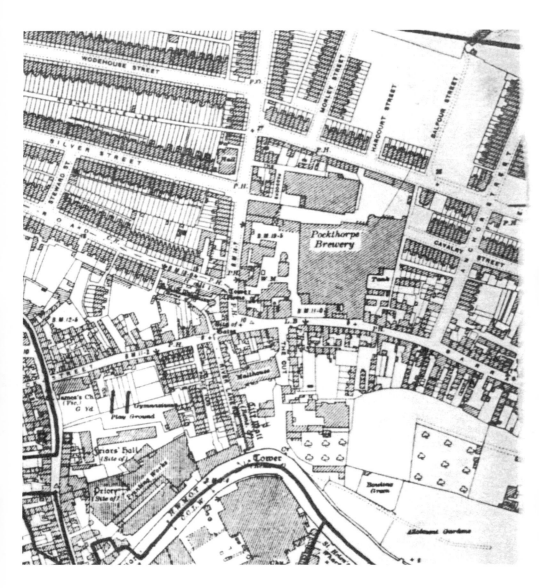

Map of north east Norwich in 1914 (1928 edition)

Copyright: Norfolk Record Office DCN 26/57

Part One

CHILDHOOD

The family photograph

1. My Parents

We had this lovely photo of the family on our living room wall. That's just a shame I wasn't there, but it was taken in 1913, the year before I was born. I think Mother was so proud and thought: 'Well that's my lot. I've finished with having babies. We'll have a family photo and that'll be it.' And then she must have fell with me directly after. I don't know what happened. Father was drunk again, I reckon. Anyhow, on December 23, 1914, mother had me, her seventeenth child.[1] My sisters told me how she sat up in bed after I was born, scrubbing handkerchiefs and washing socks in a bowl, with me beside her. I don't remember my sisters saying mother was worried about having me or anything like that, but my little brother Charlie, they say he spit on me when he saw me.

---

[1] Why did Ethel's parents have so many children? One part of the answer is that birth control products were too expensive for working people at the turn of the century. French letters, as condoms were then called, generally cost about half a crown for three. This would have broken many household budgets or, put another way, would have cost a man about 15 pints of beer. Beyond the cost, there was the embarrassment of buying them. Charles Robinson who began working in a chemist's shop in Norwich in the 1920s recalls how purchases were made:

'A customer who did not already know first had the embarrassment of finding out if the shop sold them. When a solitary man came in, asked loudly for a tube of toothpaste and then lingered anxiously while the girl assistants discreetly disappeared, you knew what he really wanted. The matter did not end there. When at last he eventually found the courage to lean over the counter and whisper, his requirement still had to be met. The articles were kept, no less securely than the dangerous drugs, locked in the safe next to the cash box. The junior apprentice was not really supposed to know, so the forbidden word was passed quietly along the line to one of the pharmacists. Then, with eyes averted and sometimes a slight reddening of the cheeks, he would grope blindly on the top shelf of the safe, hastily wrap something up in plain white paper, apply a blob of sealing wax, and hand it to the customer himself, saying 'take two and sixpence, Charles'. It was all very awkward.' [Robinson C.W. *Twentieth century druggist: memoirs.* Beverley: Galen Press; 1983.]

My oldest brother was Albert. 'How come Albert's name is Chaplin and our name is Edwards?' I asked my sisters. And that's how I come to hear the tale. My grandfather was wealthy. He owned a bakery in Coberg Street, and a lot of cottages nearby that he rented out.[2] He sent Mother to a private school near The Close,[3] and he wanted her to marry this posh man who wore a tall silk hat. The man had a carriage, he dressed very smart, and he liked mother. I think he was nice enough, but Mother was in love with Father. Grandfather said she wasn't to go with him, but she did. And father was a handsome little man. I've no idea where they met, but mother got pregnant with little Albert when she was seventeen. My father would have married her then, but Grandfather wouldn't let him. I think he thought there was still hope with the other man. Not that I think he would have had her once she got a baby? Mother and baby Albert lived with Grandfather. He was good to her, 'cause if a girl got pregnant in them days, she usually went to the workhouse[4] or she was slung into the street.

Grandfather never wanted Mother to marry Father. I think he knew there and then that Father wasn't going to be a lot of good, 'cause he liked to drink. Anyhow, after Mother had little Albert, she must have got back with my father, 'cause she got pregnant again. She was naughty really, to do it again, but when you get with someone you

[2] These were among the houses demolished when they built the new Caley's chocolate factory.

[3] The Close surrounds the Cathedral and is the most prestigious residential address in Norwich.

[4] See footnote p. 177

love, I suppose it can happen. Well, two illegitimate children, you can't have that. So, Mother and Father got married, but they couldn't change Albert's name. Not like you can now. It must have been sad for him at school with a different name to his brothers and sisters. Maybe that's why he wet the bed, 'cause he wet it for years, even when he was a man.

When they first got married, Father used to knock Mother about when he was drunk. My oldest sister, Clarrie, say she would hear him come home, go straight up to my mother, and hit her. And she hadn't done nothing wrong. Clarrie was frightened that Father would knock the lamp over and set the place afire, so she used to grab it up and run into the yard with it. At that time of day, it was a terrible thing for a woman when her husband hit her. She couldn't tell the policeman, and she daren't go to her own father. One time, Father give Mother two big black eyes, so she put her cloak round her head and covered them up when she went out. But when she was going past grandfather's baker's office, he ran out of the shop and whipped the cloak off and he said to her: 'Why didn't you come and see me?' Not that there was anything he could do, because in them days, you didn't interfere between a man and his wife. And anyway, Mother loved Father. She was besotted by him. But one night she thought she'd had enough of the hitting. She was a biggish woman and when Father hit her that time, she jumped up and hit him back. And he never done it no more.

I think Grandfather thought quite a lot of my father in the end. Father used to go and sit with him when he were dying. Mother said that Grandfather called for him to come the evening that he died. Just before he arrived, Grandfather got out of bed and wrote a will on the dressing table. He had money. He had property, and he wanted my mother and father to have some of it. But it weren't no good. He should have made a will long before then. That weren't a proper will what he wrote on the dressing table. Anyone could have done it. So, all what he left went to his eldest son, Mother's brother Billy. All the money, all the cottages what were in Coberg Street, and loads of houses – nice terraced houses - Billy took the lot and he didn't share it with anyone. He didn't give my mother nothing, nor any of the rest of his family. He didn't give his own wife, Aunt Sally, nothing neither. She never got a penny. Mother had no time for Uncle Billy. 'He ought to die with his boots on,' she always used to say.

Father was a smart little man, and a lovely man, when he wasn't on the drink. And Mother, oh, she was an elegant lady. All prim and proper. She wore a black blouse and a long skirt full of patches. Of course, she had her best skirt what she kept for Sundays and if she went out anywhere. Her little brooches were nothing to speak of. They were only to make sure her neck was covered. And I never see her with any ring except her wedding ring, which she always kept on. She had holes in her ears, but I never see her with earrings. And she never ever made up. I never see Mother, or any other elderly person make up. To be truthful, I don't think they had time. Her hair was normally plain. She used to have curlers in for a little while before Saturday night, but she'd never ever venture out the door in them.

Mother was always there. If we walked in the house and we didn't see her, we'd shout: 'Mother, Mother, where are you?' 'I'm only upstairs making the beds,' she'd say and she'd come down. If I brought kids home from school, they'd all have some bread and drippin'. My grown-up brothers and sisters lived up the road in the flats up Mousehold Street. And their kids used to come for food, even though their mothers were only up the top there. Mother was always loving and kind. She didn't say prayers or nothing, but she was forever thanking God for this, and thanking God for that. Everything was hard, but I never heard her complain. I know she'd swear sometimes and we'd say: 'Mother, don't swear.' 'You'd make a parson swear in his pulpit,' she said. But they weren't bad words. Just b's – ordinary words – and she had to be angry to do it. Most of the time she was singing around. She was a wonderful lady.

2. 13, Cavalry Street – my home

Streets were very different in my day. They were narrow and the paths were tiny, but you could go anywhere without being worried about getting runned over by a car. If you went up the city you might see one car, but there weren't many. I think the first car I saw properly was my sister, Clara's. (They had a piano, a bungalow at Hemsby, and a motorbike and sidecar. And then they bought a car. They always had everything, but they didn't posh up.) Of course, you had to be careful of the horses. There were horses and carts going backwards and forwards all the time. Our mothers would always be telling us: 'Be careful of the horses.' The milkman, the baker, the coal man, anyone what come round with anything had to have a horse and cart. Then there were the brewery horses with barrels of beer.

Loads of horse muck. That was one thing they didn't have to clean up from the streets. The people done that. Every morning, you'd see them coming with big pails to get their manure. They swept it up for their garden or their allotment. I remember one old fellow what I really was angry with. He was an aggressive little man and he used to chase his horse round, and whip it at the same time. Loads and loads of times I seen him do that. I used to shout: 'You old devil, you. Stop hitting it.' We used to cry at things like that when we were little.

They used to send round a wagon with water to clean our streets. Two horses and a cart, and this great big round tumble thing. They'd go all round the streets and spray water and disinfectant. And the drain cleaner come round regular. He was a big man and he had high leather boots up to his hip. I forget his name. He used to open the things up, and go right down into the drain and put stuff down.

The dustbin men used to come in a cart with two horses. They come regular. There were these big, old, hard tin bins. Oh, they were horrible. They never had no lids and there were flies all round. The bin men had to go to everyone's house and carry the bins along the lane. They had an old leather thing on their back, 'cause that was a filthy job. And they used to hump the bins on their shoulder. I should think their back must have been distorted.

Then there were the men what used to empty the toilet bins. They come with a big cart and two horses. They were different to the ordinary bin men. Someone told me they had three eyes, but I never saw them, 'cause they come in the middle of the night.[5] Probably took two men to carry a bin, 'cause it must have swirled around inside, mustn't it? Like when you carry a saucepan what's full of vegetables. The poor things should have been paid good money shouldn't they? But I bet they didn't get much. They might have been paid a shilling more than the other bin men, but I'd rather have had that shilling less. We had flush toilets on our side of the road but them what lived in that row of houses over the road; they never had a chain to pull. My friend, Maudie, lived in one. They had this wood seat with a hole in the middle, and a big old bin beneath it. It was a wide seat and you could put your hands out on it. And I thought it was lovely. I'd say: 'Maudie, I'm coming over to yours. Can I go on your lavatory?' And she say: 'Yes, if you like.' I don't know why I wanted to. It stunk horrible.

---

[5] The night soil collectors were employed by the City Council. They used to work at night, because of the fiercely bad smell of their cart.

Oh dear, oh dear. I sat on it. I smelt it. But I never thought about it. Sometimes it were nearly full to the brim, 'cause the people didn't have nowhere else to go. All the people doing it on top of the other. Terrible. Once you'd finished, you put a lid over the top, but all that filth stood for a week. Aw, it make you sick thinking about it.

There were two rows of houses in our street, terraced houses with nice lace curtains. We didn't use the front ways very much 'cause they was too special. We used to come up the back way. We had a garden, but it weren't one with flowers. Just a toilet, a shed, a bin, a drain with a crinkly, crankly bit of tin over it, and this big bench where mother stood and did her washing. Then there was a big wall, what went all the length of the garden and round. That was painted white. Mother used to put the birds' food along it every day. Even when it snowed, she'd sweep the snow away and feed them.

There were these lovely red steps up to the kitchen. They had to be scrubbed on your knees. The kitchen floor was red brick tiles, and we scrubbed them every week too. Not everyone used to whitewash the kitchen walls every Friday, but our mother did[6]. And she'd scrub the table and the windowsills. Up the corner of the kitchen, there was

---

[6] Houses were much more difficult to keep clean during Ethel's childhood. The smoke from coal fires and stoves and boilers could leave black marks on walls. Dirt and grime brought in on clothes and shoes from the dusty roads, and tobacco smoke in small living areas also left their mark. Moreover, the windows that were often left open for ventilation would bring in the residues from the coal fire smoke of all the adjoining houses and factories. In the days before vacuum cleaners, it was hard work to collect and get rid of dust rather than merely circulate it through the house. Wall surfaces could not simply be washed down. To keep a wall looking clean, frequent repainting would be necessary – hence Ethel's mother's weekly whitewash. Whitewash was cheap. It was a mixture of chalk and size diluted in water. As the mixture was spread on the wall the water would evaporate leaving the chalk adhering to the wall. Washing the wall would serve only to remove the chalk and re-expose any dirt beneath it.

a very narrow sink and a copper.[7] We used to turn the copper lid upside down when we washed up and stack the plates on it, but someone had to wipe up 'cause there wasn't enough space to put all the cups and plates there. Then there was a mangle,[8] a big old iron one, and Mother used to be glad of that. There was an oven in the wall, black, with a brass door handle. Off the kitchen there was a walk-in pantry. That had to be scrubbed each week as well. There was an old chair as you come in from the kitchen. It was a little chair with wooden arms. Underneath it, there was a wooden bar and an old cushion. I say a cushion, but we never had no cushions in our house. It must have been a bit of matting what was cut off. No one ever sat on the chair. For what reason I'll never know. Our little dog, Flossie, used to be under the chair. That's where her place was, and she rarely came out. When I was little I used to get under the chair with her, and she used to lick me all over the face.

We had linoleum on the floor in the living room, and a good mat from the second hand shop on the hearth. I can't ever remember anything raggedy in my house. We had a fender[9] and a hob,[10] black and shiny. They was done beautiful, and Mother always had a kettle

[7] The 'copper' was a metal tub that was bricked-in in a corner of the kitchen. A fire made with the cheapest combustible materials, such as newspaper soaked in paraffin followed by shreds of leather from the shoe factory, would be lit beneath the tub to boil the laundry. The copper had other uses too; boiling water for baths and for cooking shellfish and Christmas puddings.

[8] A hand-turned device for squeezing the water out of laundry

[9] A metal guard that ran around the edge of the hearth about three inches in height.

[10] A black metal extension to the coal fire that provided hot plates and an oven rather like a contemporary Aga. Obviously it was not possible to control the heat with any precision.

on the side, 'cause you always wanted hot water. When it was cold, she'd let us sit on stools round the fire when we came home from school. But when it got to a quarter to six, she'd say: 'Get away from that fire. The others will be home soon and they'll want to be warmed.' And they did. That was Mother caring for everyone. There was an old marble clock on the mantelpiece. And two big old vases with flowers on and a bit of gold round the edges. And I know what was on what I wish I'd got today – a little boy and girl in china. The boy's knickerbockers were blue with pink bows and roses all up them. And the girl was in a pink dress with blue at the front, and a big blue hat. The mantelpiece was just black, but Mother always used to have a nice fringe around it, one with all these little bobbles on it. Nearly everybody used to have a fringe round the mantelpiece. If ever Father didn't go out at night, he'd sit by the fire, smoking. He'd get a big bit of paper to light his cigarette and sometimes he'd catch this lovely little fringe. Then he'd have to get up and clap the fire out. But poor Mother had to go and get a new fringe didn't she, 'cause she wouldn't have her mantelpiece without one. Over the fireplace there was the big family picture. The one what I'm not in. I don't think she had any other photos of us.

⊰⊱

In the summer, we had a flypaper up. Absolutely full of flies it was. You couldn't get a pinprick on it. But you had to get as many flies as you could on it, 'cause you couldn't afford another. We always had a nice chenille cloth on the table. So, it always looked cosy. A lot of people just had newspaper, specially them what lived in the yards.[11]

[11] The 'yards' (from courtyards) were the areas of slum housing close to Ethel's house. See p.85-90.

But our mother wouldn't have no paper on her table. It was a big one, but I don't know how she got us all round. Father had one of them big old wood armchairs. We all respected that chair. It was like a throne really. When he was home, no one was allowed to sit on it but him. But when he wasn't there, it was ours, and we all had a turn. Of course, the minute we saw him coming up the road, we got out. Mother used to have to sit on an ordinary upright chair. The older ones sat on plain wood chairs or stools, and for us kids, there was a plank what went between two chairs with the backs off. Us young ones used to sit up there, but if brother Frank got up at any time, the other end would go up, 'cause he was so fat and heavy. We didn't fall on the floor, 'cause as soon as he knew, he corrected it, but we had a jerk. Never had a soft chair in the house really. We did have a couch. It wasn't rent. It was all in good order, but I never seen Mother sit on it. Too low for her I should think. I used to play rich ladies on it. With a curtain round me, and earrings and beads. Imaginary mind I had when I was a little girl.

Mother used to scrub the front door step till it shone, and she always had a nice doormat where you came in. Nothing shoddy, no bits of old rag mat, nor nothing like that. The front room was always cooler when you walked through. We only had a fire in there but once a year at Christmas. It was what you called the never-used-room really. It was for high days and holidays, or when someone died.[12] The

---

[12] To have a room that was reserved for special occasions conferred a certain status that was very important. It distinguished families living with Ethel in Cavalry Street from the poorer people in the smaller houses in the nearby 'yards'. In his 1910 study of life in Norwich, Hawkins noted: 'The front parlour is almost a universal cult in Norwich, jealously preserved for the Family Bible and the stuffed birds and miscellaneous crockery without which no man can be respectable. Except on rare occasions it is never used to sit in, still less to play or sleep in.'

**Cavalry Barracks, Norwich, which gave its name to Cavalry Street.
Ethel could see the soldiers from her window.**

people had a cuppa tea and a bit o' cake in the front room when they
come to pay their respects. It had a bay window, with beautiful,
beautiful, crisp, white lace curtains. Mother never had curtains what
you pulled, just a blind, about one and six from Price's.[13] She kept her
sewing machine under the window, and a fuschia in a big green bowl
on top of it. There was linoleum on the floor, all polished, and a lovely
mat in front of the hearth. Every so often, Mother would say: 'I'll get
myself another mat,' and off she'd go to the second hand shop. The
mats what she got come from ladies' houses. It was all paid in cash.
Bless her heart, she didn't like having debts. On one wall she had a big
frame with these silk cards: 'To mother from your son', all done in
needlework. The brothers what were in the war had sent them. And

[13] See p.115

she had a photo of her father, great big old face and sideburns. There was a picture what hung over the hearth – lovely that was – a woman wearing a gold crucifix round her neck. She was like a beautiful, golden-haired, lavender angel. The mantelpiece was black polished marble with a nice black fender. The fender in the living room we were always cleaning, but the one in the front room we cleaned but once a year.

I don't know where all the furniture in the front room came from. I expect my grandfather give 'em some. There was this lovely polished sideboard, and a mahogany table and six chairs. The legs were all curved. They were like red china when you looked at them. And up the corner from the fire was this shelf. It took up the whole corner. There were glass dishes on it, with crinkly edges. And a tea service in lovely china, white with blue and gold rims. Things what you wouldn't use every day, but if anyone come she'd bring them out. Plates, saucers, cups and a sugar basin and a jug to match. You could see Mother had standards. Everything always went back in the right order. I never remember breaking anything. We must have been so careful, 'cause we knew they were something we couldn't replace.

We didn't have any light in the kitchen or upstairs, but we had gaslight in the living room, and of course we had it in the front room too[14]. On Christmas morning, Mother would get up early and light the front room, because they'd all be coming and going. But the light in the living room was the main one. They used to have little chains on

[14] Gas lighting appeared in Norwich workers' homes from the mid-nineteenth century, although families could rarely afford to have it fitted in all rooms. Household electricity did not become available until the turn of the twentieth century and was not installed in workers' homes until the 1920s and 30s.

the lights. You put 'em up if you wanted it brighter or down, if you wanted it a bit low. Mother had to light the filament herself. You see, Father was never there, and she wouldn't let us do it, 'cause it was dangerous. She had to stand on a chair to do it. It was only like a cobweb really. She'd be lighting this thing and sometimes the match would catch the filament and go through it. Then the gas would all ooze out. 'Oh,' she'd say. 'That's a b. in't it?' It made her angry, 'cause she'd have to find three ha'pence, and send one of us over the road to Mrs Howlett's to get a new one. (We got electric lights when I was about ten years old.)

I never see a candle in my house. No, that was too dangerous. I heard of a boy who lived in a row near us. I think he was about twelve. He took a candle to the toilet at the bottom of the garden. And when he was on the toilet, he got burned to death. If he shouted, no one heard him. In wintertime, we had to go upstairs in the dark and come down in the dark. I was terrified. When my father said: 'Get my boots from under the bed,' my heart used to start beating. He used to come home filthy, see, so he had to change when he wanted to go out. Why he couldn'ta got his boots when he got his suit I can't understand. Summer time were alright, but winter! It was pitch black. I used to wait for it. He'll ask me in a minute, I thought. And I couldn't refuse. You always did what you were told, even if you were petrified. My heart went thump-thump-thump. I used to lump up them stairs and bang my feet as loud as I could. I wonder why my mother didn't say: 'What you doing?' Then I used to race down with the boots. I'd miss a couple of steps. I could have broke my neck. There was no banister to hold on to. But I was frightened of the devil coming after me. 'The old devil'll get you if you aren't good,' they used to say.[15] 'He'll burn you up.' They frightened kids in them days.

Mother's bedroom had a chest of drawers and one of them mirrors on a swivel. She always had a beautiful feather bed with white sheets and a white blanket with a blue stripe through it. And she had a nice white counterpane. I used to love getting in bed with her. If we weren't well, she'd put us in there for a bit. When we were right little, she'd keep us there all night. The other two bedrooms never had nothing much in. In the girls' room, we had a tin trunk, where Edie and Rose put all their fancy things. And beds – two in the boys' room and one in ours. Top and bottom people were sleeping. We were all sharing. There were four of us to the bed in my time, but they must have had more before I was born when there were more children at home. Me and Nelly were at the bottom of the bed 'cause we were the youngest. The thing is that when the older ones came to bed, we'd be lovely and warm and then they'd open up the bed and upset everything. Sometimes they got their foot in your face, but you'd push it away. I can't remember losing any sleep over it. We got a lot of exercise, and we were really tired when we got to bed.

Mother used to have clean sheets on the bed every week. They smelt beautiful. Even though we were poor, we had sheets and pillowcases. She used to buy this calico to make them. When she bought it, it was kind of browny, but after she boiled it once or twice, it used to come up like snow. I don't know how she had time to do it. Mind you she didn't have no telly to watch, nor no gramophone. We never had

---

15 When Ethel was a child, it was quite normal to instill fear into children by saying the devil or various bogeymen would come to get them if they were disobedient.

anything like that. There was no heating were there, but we had army blankets what the boys brought home from the 1914 war. Brown with a red stripe running through, and army coats on top of them if it were extra cold. With all our bodies we soon got warm. We were too many in a bed to be cold. And then we had a great stone water bottle. Whoever went to bed first would have it. Mother would rub it round the bed and then she'd bring it down and fill it up again. (Poor old girl, she was up and down the stairs all the while. But she didn't think of herself.) The last one who had the bottle kicked it out when it was cold, and you'd hear a thump in the night.

3. Home Life

In my day, men were the head of the house and what they said went. Father had everything done for him. He was waited on hand and foot. When he was at home, none of the boys didn't get out of line. But mostly he weren't there. By the time he come home, the little kids were all snug in bed.

One day, my sister Nelly said to me: 'Oooh, Father want you. You done something terrible.' I couldn't remember what I'd done wrong, but when your father wanted to see you, you had to jump. There was no two ways about it. When I got indoors, I said: 'Father want me?' And my mother said: 'What you talking about? Father in't home from work yet. Go on with you. Get out and play.' Nelly could be very nasty when we were little. She'd say: 'No one like you.' And I used to think, why don't they like me? A few years ago, she told me: 'I couldn't bear you when we were little. Everyone was loving you and giving you things. I weren't much older and I wasn't getting anything'. I didn't think anything of it at the time, but she was right. My brother Graham and his wife Ethel bought me a little pram and a doll. I found it in the front room, under the shelf with the china, when they came to visit one Saturday afternoon. I thought it was marvellous, but poor Nelly, she didn't get nothing. Even so, we were great mates. We were always together. The first thing I remember is standing on a stool, watching Nelly going off to school for the first time and crying: 'I want my Lelly.'

Mother was the one what dealt with us. She used to say: 'Now you all love each other. None of you quarrel in this house. If you start that, I'll bang all your heads together.' We'd be laughing and joking. Then all of a sudden, she'd get fed up with it. She'd come and give us all a clout. She used to say: 'I'll get the right one, if I give you all one.' You'd get a clip, not round the ear hole, but the side of your face. And it was a good one, not just a tap. Cor, that made you shut up. I didn't do much, 'cause I was little. But the boys, up to everything they were. I used to hear my mother say: 'I'll swing for you'.[16] And I thought: 'What does she mean? I don't want Mother to be hung.'

Mother was strait-laced. Sometimes the girls and boys would be there in the evening. And they'd be joking and laughing, 'cause there was none of the wireless thing. My sisters would be sitting there, and perhaps one of their skirts would ride up a bit over the knee, 'cause they wore short things in the 1920s. And Mother would say: 'Rosie, pull your skirt down. You ought to be ashamed in front of your brothers.' One day, after tea, two or three boys come round after my brother Sam. They knocked at the door and they come in, 'cause the door was always undone. And one of these young men – I don't think he were above sixteen – he sort of smacked Mother on the behind. Well, she no more to do, but punched him and knocked him clean out. It so offended her that she just instinctive did it. My sister told me that my brother was walking him round the block to get him round. He dursen't[17] stay in the house. Well, he didn't mean anything by it, but you see that's the sort of woman Mother was. She wouldn't do anything that wasn't right and she wouldn't have no one doing to her what wasn't right. Later on, the young man came and said he was

---

[16] In other words, I'll murder you even if it means I'll be caught and hanged and left swinging on the end of the rope.

[17] did not dare

sorry. Mother accepted his apology and he had bread and cheese and a cup of cocoa with us. But it was a vile thing to happen in my house. Though we were a big family, we were well behaved.

Mother didn't get angry with us much. Most of the time she was too busy preparing food and washing and scrubbing to even think about us lot. What a life. All them children in a little terraced house. It must have been very hard. But she did have some wonderful times when they grew up. They all used to come round to see her. Brother Billy and brother Graham used to come on a Saturday and give her a shilling, which was quite a lot. Plus Billy used to bring her Mintoes.[18] She kept them in the cupboard and I used to go and nick one now and again.

Mother was up at six every morning, 'cause she had to light the fire. Sometimes she had to chop the wood an' all. I could never understand why with all them boys around. Us little kids never came down until the older ones had gone to work. We'd dress upstairs and wash our face and hands at the sink. We weren't really dirty 'cause in the evening before we went to bed we had a big bowl on a stool and we always washed our arms and necks and all that. The fire was lovely by the time we got up. Sometimes I wouldn't be dressed and I'd tuck my feet in my red flannel nightie and sit in front of the flames.

Mother would cut a lot of bread off for breakfast. We had a choice: marge or dripping[19] or cheese. She tried to get the fire just right, but after one or two toasts there'd be a little bit of cinder that'd go on the cheese. Well, a bit of coal really. 'Ooh, there's a b.,' she'd say. She

---

[18] Boiled sweets with a peppermint buttery flavour.

[19] The fat that had dripped from roasting meat and been left to solidify, commonly used for spreading on bread or toast.

just used to get a knife and whack it off and we'd eat it. She couldn't afford to throw it away. We always had a cuppa tea. That was very weak, but that was sweet and we liked it. And we didn't just have breakfast. We took two rounds of bread and dripping for lunch.[20] Never had no biscuits or anything like that. We wouldn't even dream on 'em. We had the basics.

The whole family come home for dinner. I was home before the older ones. Mother had a nice chenille cloth in the day, but when she set the table for dinner it was a blue checked cloth during the week and a white one on Sunday. She always had a lovely cooked meal for us. You sat up there and you all ate properly 'cause it was all respect. You couldn't say you didn't want. You didn't have no choice. You wouldn't even think of it. And when you were up at the table, you didn't naff about. There was never any talking or running on at meal times, because everyone was too busy eating. We were always hungry. There was never nothing over, but I can't never say I got away from the table and wished I had more. Mother got the food what was good for us, and we ate it. She must have been a good manager. I don't know how she done it, the old girl.

One day a week we had pea soup. Mother boiled it up with a hoof of pork. Oh that was delicious. The peas all used to go to nothing. One day we had meat patties, and another day we'd have meat dumplings. We'd go to the butcher and say: 'Give us a couple o' penn'orth of suet,' and he'd rend off a great lump. There was skin in between and Mother had to get it out. Then she'd grate it. Oh, her meat dumplings were out of this world. The grown-ups had them in

---

[20] Lunch was a mid-morning snack. Dinner was eaten in the middle of the day. Tea was eaten when everyone came home from school or work.

basins, but us kids had them in saucers. There weren't a lot of gravy, because the saucer didn't hold much, but that was nourishing, 'cause that was suet. Mother was very selective about her meat. We never had no mince, always proper meat. I remember her saying after we'd had dinner one time: 'I'll have to tell the butcher. That weren't up to my usual standard.' She always kept them on their toes. The night before she made steak and kidney pudding, she'd get us to cut the meat up. Once a week we'd have a piece of skirt[21] what was ever so cheap. If you liked fat, you could eat it, and it made beautiful gravy. Fridays Mother got liver. She used to fry it up and a bit of sausage and an egg. So each day we always had a good meal.

After dinner, the older ones went back to work and the kids went to school. Mother used to then sit with her feet on the fender. I seen her do it lots o' times. She'd just sit there on an ordinary wooden chair with her hands on her knees. One day, the kettle was boiling and the water boiled over – on both her feet, not one. And her sitting there and going: 'Oooh!' I couldn't have started school, 'cause I was there with her. She had her old black stockings on. And she had to get them off. I can remember her getting the scissors and pouring some scalding water over them to sterilize them. And these blisters, two on each foot come up. Blisters as big as sausages. She cut them and let the water out. She didn't make no fuss. She put a bandage round and carried on working. Oh, I can't believe it. She never made a deen.[22]

In them days, a lot of people went home to bread and butter for tea. They had a dinnertime meal and that was it. But our mother

---

[21] Skirt is a cheap cut of beef taken from just below the diaphragm of the cow. It is best suited for braising.

[22] never made a sound

wouldn't dream of that, being brought up like she was. She done what her mother done. We always had a lovely tea, something she'd cooked.[23] She wore a coloured apron when she was cleaning, but at tea time the white apron would always come out. And of course, there was always a tablecloth. I don't remember spilling anything on it. I think we were all too close together.

Tuesdays it were hoof of pork for tea. Mother would take the hoof out of the pea soup and cut it up. She'd sit there, dishing it out on all these plates. It wouldn't have went that far with all of us. But we'd run over to the shop with a couple of glasses, the sort what you drink out of, and we'd get two penn'orth of pickled onions and a couple o' penn'orth of cabbage. The onions was in big jars and they smelt beautiful. And you knew Mrs Howlett would fill up your glasses. We'd finish them all off with the pork. There were so many of us. And Mother would give us a bit of tomato and cucumber. And vinegar. We didn't have no sauce in them days, but always loads of bread and butter. Sometimes, Mother made her own pork cheeses[24] in a little basin. They were brown and got onion in. I think they were the hoof of pork, melted down. I never liked them.

Fridays, it were usually cockles and mussels for tea. Mother used to do her own. She'd be there, sitting at the table when I come home from school, a big pail beside her. She'd open them and put a little flour in them. They said that fattened 'em up. She'd throw the shells

[23] This was unlikely to have been the case a few years earlier when most of the children were still dependents. When Ethel was born six of her siblings were working but still living at home. Their wages would have had a significant impact on the family budget.

[24] Pork cheese is also known as brawn. It is generally made by boiling a pig's head with herbs and seasoning, then separating the meat from the bones and leaving it to set into a hard jelly. Sometimes, pigs' trotters (feet) were used.

in the pail and then she'd have two big stone dishes, one for the cockles and one for the mussels. She had to light the copper and boil them up in that. And then after, she had to clean it all out, so it was ready to heat the water for our bath. That was all work for her, but when you've a big family to feed, you can't just do one basin full. We had the cockles and mussels with salt, pepper and vinegar. Every little while, I see Mother stuff one in her mouth. I suppose she didn't get a lot of food. She had too much to do. Sister Edie loved Mother's mussels. I can see her now sitting up at the table, next to Rose. Edie always used to give me a penny on a Friday evening.[25] So I'd be there, standing waiting. I wanted to get up the street to Sally and Thursy's and buy me a ha'pence worth of sweets. But would she give me that till she'd had her mussels? No. I had to wait till she'd supped every one down.

From time to time, Mother got bloaters from Howard's, the fish shop. But more often than not, she used to get crabs. The eldest ones, the ones that were working, they used to have a full crab. Mother couldn't afford one for each of us, but she'd keep a couple back for us kids to share. She used to put pepper and vinegar with them and we used to have the bottoms spread on bread. Lots of beautiful bread. And then we were allowed to have all the little claws. We used to crack them with our teeth and suck that little thing at the bottom. Oh, we were well away.

A good crab was five pence. Oh yes, for five pence you could get one of the really elite. But now and again Mother'd say to me: 'Here's a penny, go and get yourself a watery crab.' That was when some

[25] Wages were paid every Friday in cash.

water had got in while it was being boiled. I used to clean it in the street. I knew how to do it, 'cause I'd watched Mother. And then I'd suck it. Even though they were watery, they were still lovely.

So every day we all sat up and had a proper tea, even though we'd been home and had a dinner. I don't think Mother ever ate a lot. But she did use to like a bit of bread with a thick bit of butter on it. I can remember her putting a little salt on and loving it. I think she used to get half a pound from an old lady what come round with the vegetables. It come in a roll. Of course, she didn't have it all to herself. She wouldn't do that. Crusty bread we had. Beautiful bread. Oh, I can taste it now.[26]

Mother tried to please everybody with her food, but especially Albert. Poor Albert. I think he must have suffered because he didn't have his father's name. He always seemed a bit sad. Mother would say to Nelly: 'Oh Albert will be home in a minute,' and she'd send her to get the special food what he used to like – ducks' giblets. She used to have to go to a special place on the market to get them. So that was all additional to what Mother had to do for us. And I used to think, why's Mother got to worry about that? Why don't Albert have food like us?

Father used to like a bit of fish, so on Wednesday evenings, Mother would have some bread and butter ready, and a little corner of the table set. She'd say to us: 'Father'll be home for his bit of skate tonight.' I used to love that, 'cause you knew that he weren't going to

---

[26] The bread probably did taste better in Ethel's childhood when bakers used traditional methods of letting the bread rise before baking it. The bread tasted good but needed eating quickly before it became stale. Today's industrial processes of making bread use hydrolyzed oils and extra salt to do away with the waiting time for the bread to rise. This speeds up the production process and produces bread that will keep fresh for several days, but, often, at the expense of taste.

stay out late that night. He weren't going to come home drunk, and mother weren't going to get angry and shout at him. I never saw him hit her, but it was the shouting. He was home by quarter to ten, and as soon as he got in the door, one of us would run to the fish shop. You could get a nice bit of skate for four pence.

⚜

On a Friday night, all of us young ones used to go in the bath. Mother would light the old copper up, 'cause we didn't have hot water, and a kettle wouldn't bath you. We had a huge bath that Mother hung on the coal shed door. She used to carry it into the house. I can't understand how she did it by herself. She'd scoop the hot water out of the copper with a round metal thing with a wood handle. Next she'd put in a little soda. We used to be like little lobsters when we come out. Mind you, I don't think it did us any harm, and we were all rosy and clean. She didn't just put one in the bath and throw the water out. She used to do all us in the same bath. I used to be first to go in. I suppose Mother say: 'Let the baby get in first.' If the boys wanted to come in the house when we were in the bath, they had to come in the front door and sit in the front room 'cause there was no privacy otherwise. I think they had a bath after we did, all boys together.

Little Sam, my brother Sam's boy, he fell in a hot bath one time. They lived in a one-bedroomed flat up Mousehold Street. It was Friday evening, and his mother was bathing her little ones. And Sammy, I think he was seven or eight, he stood on a chair next to the bath, which was stupid. And stupid again, because his mother didn't put cold water in first. Our mother always used to do the cold first, and then the hot, and keep testing it. But little Sam's mother brought scalding hot water and put it in the bath. I suppose he was playing around and he fell in backwards. He was scalded from the neck downwards. Oh, she was all upset my mother was. 'The stupid woman,' she say. 'Whatever sense has she got? Putting in the hot water before the cold.' So that was a terrible thing. He was in hospital for weeks, and he stuttered when he came out.

Mother used to wash her hair regular. It was very dark. It never went grey. She'd then braid it and she used to look like a new pin. I don't think she ever went in the bath. She was too big. She used to put her feet in a big bowl. And she'd have her clothes up to her knees, and wash her feet. After, she used to go upstairs with the bowl and wash all her other parts. She was spotless, really spotless. But before she went to Mr Dawson's, the butcher in Magdalen Street she'd always wash her feet and legs, and put clean stockings on. You see, she didn't want to be like Mrs C., who had an accident down Barrack Street. It was the talk of all the street that her feet were black as soot. Everyone was talking about them, even though you can bet half of them had black feet, themselves. But not my mother. Her legs were lily white.

I can't remember even seeing a toothbrush in my house when I was little. We wouldn't have known which one to use with all us lot. When we wanted to clean our teeth we used to go to the chimney and put our finger up to get some soot. We'd rub it along our teeth and then rinse it off. All that stuff on your teeth and in your mouth. Horrible taste. It was all grit, but it used to clean our teeth as white as snow. We wanted our teeth to look smart and that's how we did it.[27]

[27] Using soot or powdered burnt toast was a common way of cleaning teeth in Victorian times. Toothbrushes and tins of hard dentifrice became available from the 1870s, but they would have been expensive for a working family.

Mother washed our hairs the night before we had a bath. She used to take the cloth off the living room table and put a bowl on it. She used a soft brown soap that came in a tin. It looked like brown treacle, and it smelt horrible.[28] But that got a lovely lather. Oil of sassafras, what stank horrible, she then put that on. I used to hate it 'cause I thought the children at school would smell it. Mother would say: 'You can tell them at school that your mother's cleaning your hair before you get fleas.' Every week, after she'd washed all our hairs, she'd go through them for fleas and nits. She wore an apron, and she'd tuck the bottom into the back of our necks. Not the white one she had up at the table, a blue check one. First she got the small toothcomb, and one or two fleas would fall out into the apron. They were head lice really, but we used to call them fleas. Once you got the fleas in your hair, they were making nits all the while, so if she didn't get them out, you were full of head fleas the next morning. The nits were little pearl eggs and you had to pull them off. It was a long drawn out thing and it took ages. You couldn't just get a hair and say: 'There's four nits here,' and pull them all out. You had to get your two fingers and drag them out one at a time. Of course, it was the long hair what made it worse. My brothers used to do their own. I seen them put the tooth comb through and a nit drop out. Oh, they used to drop heavy on the table. We had to eat off that table, but it was all covered with newspaper when we were getting the nits out. Mother kept us clean, but it'd only be one or two weeks before we had more. You'd never be free from them, 'cause there was so many in the school. Every house had 'em.

---

[28] Commercially-prepared shampoos did not come onto a mass market until the 1930s. Most families used their own recipes, adding ingredients such as egg yolks or ammonia to soapy water. Oil of Sassafras was used to combat head lice.

There was a lot of people in them days what didn't care for their little'uns, didn't even clean the poor little kids.

Mother used to machine a lot. She made her own curtains. As you came down the hill you could see them up at the window, lovely white lace curtains. She'd make all sorts of things: aprons for herself and for us, nightdresses, petticoats, knickers, and vests. That was only a bit of flannelette with a round neck cut so you could get your head through. She used to go and get the remnants from Price's. You could sometimes pick up a bit of material for sixpence, red flannelette sometimes. No matter what colour it was, if she could get the material, she'd make shirts. For the boys, not the grown-ups; they'd buy theirs, them old working ones with a stripe and no collar. There weren't no collars on to go to work.

Mother was always mending, and sometimes she ran out of black cotton, so she had to use white. Even though the cotton reels were only a penny, she didn't always have the money to get one. She mended everything: shirts, socks, boys' trousers. Father and the older boys couldn't go and buy new Sunday shirts all the time, so she turned the collars when they wore out. She darned our socks, and when they got bad, she got another pair and 'feeted' 'em. Yes, if she could get away with it, she'd feet 'em. You know, cut the foot out of one sock and sew in the foot from another. They weren't shaped. Whatever must they have looked like? But rather that than have holes. Holes were an embarrassment.

There were some mothers what never patched. Maybe they didn't have the cotton and the needle. You don't know, do you? But there were a lot of poor kids what used to go in rags. You could see the bums through their trousers, their naked little behinds, walking through Barrack Street. There was all them boys in our family, but our mother wouldn't have their little bums showing. Even when they were growing up, she used to patch their trousers. One of my brothers – I think it was Charlie – was called out in assembly one day. 'Can you see this boy?' the headmaster said. 'Well, look at the marvellous job his mother done on his pants. He's full of patches, but at least his mother keep him warm.'

⚜

Mother was always doing something. On Mondays and Tuesdays, she was washing and that old copper had to be started. So out'd come the leather shreds. It was supposed to have been coal, but who could afford that? You could have the shreds from the boot and shoe operatives, for nothing. They were the bits what was left after they'd cut the soles and uppers out. Someone would sweep them up at night and put 'em in sacks. Mother used to send the boys up to Southall's and Chiddick's at the top of Silver Road to get them. It was a long way to go really, up all them hills and then to carry them down. I think you had to pay a little for the sacks, but they weren't the rough sacks like you see now. Mother used to boil them up and cut them up like towels. Then she'd have them hanging on the door for the boys when they come home from work to wipe themselves on before they used the clean towel.

To start the old copper, she'd shove the shreds and the paper and one or two bits of wood in. Then she'd pour in the paraffin, throw a match in, and shut the door. It'd go 'vooooom', but she never seemed afraid of anything like that. She'd fill the copper with water and while that was heating, she'd perhaps make the beds. Then, as soon as the water was boiling, she'd put tons of soda in, scoop it out with a pail, and put it in the two baths outside. She couldn't have them inside. The kitchen weren't big enough. It didn't matter about the cold weather, even when it was snowing or raining. She used to have one bath on a bench. And then she'd have another bigger bath on the ground. She scrubbed every single thing with a scrubbing brush on the scrubbing board before she put it in the bath. She done all the shirts first. Men didn't have a shirt on every day like they do now. They just had one Sunday shirt and one weekday shirt. But there was all them boys. She scrubbed the collars and cuffs especially hard, 'cause they got really dirty. And then she did all them sheets. Once the shirts and the linen had been washed in the first go, she'd wring 'em tight. Then she'd rub them with Watson's soap and throw them in the other bath to 'seconds' them, to make them so they would come a bit cleaner still. I don't think that were necessary, really. When they come out of the second bath, she rubbed 'em with her hands. Then, once she'd wrung them out, she put more soap on them and put them in the copper.

And it weren't just the washing. She were looking after the copper as well, weren't she? She had to do that all the time, see. Any old things what she could find to burn. That's why there weren't a lot of old things about in our house, 'cause they were all burned up. Rags, old boots and shoes what'd been thrown out, she'd stick them all up the copper. She'd make sure the old thing was roaring and then she'd put the lid on. After she'd finished boiling the things they were full of soap, so she then had to rinse them. She got them out with a stick and put them in the sink in cold water. And that was only a little sink. I don't know how she done the sheets. One at a time, she'd rinse the things. Then she'd take them back outside to this big bath of blue. Always cold water. It had to be done. Hail, rain, blow or snow, she'd be out there scrubbing. She'd swish the blue bag around in the water. And keep squeezing it. One bag would last for about three washes, and the things used to come out of that as white as the driven snow. And then at the end, she had to do all the handkerchiefs. And when I say handkerchiefs, I mean handkerchiefs. They weren't them paper ones. The grown-ups had proper handkerchiefs, and us kids used to have the flour bags. We had no end of them and they were lovely and soft for your nose. Sometimes, Mother would get a stool out for me and give me some soapy water, and she'd let me do the hankies and the tea towels. I used to feel I was a married woman.

The house smelt of burning paper and shreds on laundry day. Poor old Mother. When she'd finished the washing, she had to clean the copper out. All the bits were flying about and it was full of ashes. Then she had to scrub the kitchen floor, 'cause it were mucky. And the steps. She done them an' all.

The mangle was just as you come in the door to the kitchen. I used to love that old mangle, but one or two people had accidents. They'd be going so quick, they caught their finger in it. But it was really good, took nearly every bit of water out. Everything went through it. Mother didn't have to iron the towels. She just put them through the mangle and they looked beautiful. And the tea-cloths and the socks, she didn't have to iron them either. And then she had to hang it all out. We had a line from the steps to the gate, and another from the house to the gate. In winter I've seen the shirts like statues, and the towels and the pillowslips, all frozen. On days when it rained, she used to hang things round the fire. Everything had to be dry by ironing day. All that hard work before she even got to the ironing.

The washing used to smell horrible, all that dirty linen. But I remember coming home from school on Wednesdays and smelling the ironing. It had a lovely fresh smell, like walking through a field. The iron were just an ordinary heavy iron. There was nothing you put in it. Mother heated it up and spat on it to see if it was hot enough. If it spitted out, that meant it was extra hot. She heated it up on the fire and that's how it sometimes got dirty. She had a tray of something like sandpaper to clean it. Mostly, she ironed up the shirts and my father's cheat[29] beautiful, all starched. But sometimes there'd be a little bit of black go on the cheat or the shirt. 'Oh,' she'd say, 'there's a b.' And she had to wash it again. She wouldn't leave the black on it. She had a big line in the living room, 'cause there was nowhere else to air them. There'd be all shirts hanging up. They used to look lovely. I think she had 'em up about a day. But as soon as she took the clothes off, she took down the line, so it didn't look poverty-stricken.

Most women took washing in, poor things. Mother used to take in things from The Close. The clergymen all had stiff fronts and some kind of collar. They were purely religious things. Clara used to go and get them for her. First she washed them and then she had to starch them. That wasn't spray like we have today. Oh no. You had to make it up in a big bowl, and then you put your things in and wrung them out. And then she had to iron them. Poor old darling. I think she got tuppence.

---

[29] A cheat was a white panel attached to a collar that men would wear over the front of their shirts. They were heavily starched and worn on Sundays or on special occasions such as weddings and funerals. They looked like the formal dress shirts of today.

The older girls used to scrub the yard down. When I was about ten, I would do the windows, the outsides an' all. We had bay windows what pulled up. I used to sit out on the sill, and pull the window down on my knees tight. That's how I cleaned them outside windows. You had to make sure that bottom window were right tight on your knees or you would have fallen out backwards when you stretched. But Mother let me do it, and I never thought about it. Poor old girl. She was sort of big by the time I came along. I can never remember her thin. She couldn't really have got out of the window, but she wouldn't just sit there while we worked. She'd do the bottom ones.

As soon as we were old enough, we had to clean the fender. And I don't mean just once or twice a week; it was nearly every day. I don't know why we had to do it so many times. And it was always so hot, 'cause the fire never went out all day. We used to get a saucer with the black lead in it and put a little vinegar in so that was moist. We had two black lead brushes. We put the stuff on with one. The other was a three cornered one, so you could get a good shine with it. Mother used to say: 'Put some elbow grease into it.' But I didn't understand. I thought that was some grease you put on your elbows. When I come out of it, there'd be smears of black lead all over my face, and I were filthy dirty. Even my sweat was black. But I enjoyed it, 'cause at the finish, the fender was like black ebony.

Everything had to be scrubbed every week, the stools, the chairs, and not just the tops. There was all them legs. And the cupboards had to be clean, and the tins what she used for cooking things. They were all spotless. And the old knife box was there with all the knives and forks. On Friday evenings, Mother used to get my brothers to do them with bath brick.[30] They didn't do much in the house, but they done enough. The bath brick was hard. Like cement really. One of the boys scrubbed the knives and forks on it. Another had a bowl of water and washed them. And then someone used to wipe them. Mother used to cook on the living room table. But after she'd rolled all the dough for the patties, she'd get a bowl of soapy water and scrub the table and it'd be as white as white. Then, once it had dried, she'd put the chenille cloth over it.

'Can I stay at home Friday and do the bedroom floors?' I'd say to Mother every little while, 'cause I didn't like school. And she'd say: 'Well, I should think that would be all right,' 'cause she didn't bother. You had a scrubbing brush, a bucket of scalding water with bicarbonate of soda, and carbolic soap. You couldn't move the beds, so you had to get right under each one and make sure that every inch of the wood floor was cleaned, and that you'd scrubbed round all the legs. It was easier for a little person. And the old wooden stairs. You used to have a pail between your legs and scrub each one. They were scrubbed so much they were as white as snow them stairs. One time I done the stairs with the water I'd done the bedroom with and I got severely told off. 'You in't been down for clean water, have you?' she said. And of course, I had to say no. 'Go on. Go and get some clean water and go over it again,' she said. I didn't think they were that dirty, 'cause they were done every week, but that was Mother's way. So, I never made that mistake again. I don't think I ever done her room. She must have done that herself. It had linoleum, her bedroom, so I think she just used to sweep it.

---

[30] Bath bricks were bricks made from fine clay. They were used for cleaning in the way that scouring pads are used today.

My sisters were all good housewives, but even after they were married Mother would say something if she thought they were out of line. She wouldn't shout. She'd look down on them with scorn. One of my sisters-in-law, Sam's wife, Laura, she used to come down to Mother's instead of being in her own little house, keeping it clean. And she wouldn't think about going home till dinnertime. Well, the day was half gone then, wasn't it? Mother would think to herself, why aren't you doing your own work? But she wouldn't tell her. She'd tell my sisters if they were out of line, but she wouldn't put her nose in her daughter-in-law's business. And she wouldn't say nothing to Sam about it neither.

Mother's sister Clara didn't have the standards like Mother. I remember Mother going up London one time to visit her. I fretted for her while she was gone, and I suppose my mind went all funny. I remember that the first night I went to bed, I woke up. I had been sleeping and I was up the ceiling, down the ceiling, and there was all lights and things in front of my eyes. It was really horrifying. It went on for some time. And that repeated itself for two or three nights. I expect that was because I was fretful for Mother. But you can't imagine that a little child could go into that sort of state, with just a Mother leaving her for three days. I mean I weren't alone. I had grown-up sisters and brothers. And I had my dad there an' all. But that was a really, really horrible experience for me. When Mother come home, she say: 'I never seen nothing like it. I had to clean all the house before I sat down. There was cockerels messing on the copper and all round, and I couldn't stick it.

4. Sundays

I used to love Sundays. As usual, Mother got up at six to light the fire. It took her a good hour to get it going, and so we'd all be awake by the time she come upstairs with her big tray. It weren't no good her having one of them tiny trays 'cause that weren't just like she was bringing one cup of tea up. That was a whole tray full of drinks. However she got up with all them, I don't know. But we thought nothing of it. Bless her heart, she should have been in bed and we should have been getting her a cup of tea. But that's the way she was.

We had half an egg and a half a sausage for Sunday breakfast. And mother always used to fry a bit of steak. That was for the wage earners, but us kids used to get a little bit, as big as an oxo. Mother boiled marrowbones and put the juice from them in the gravy, and we could all have as much gravy as we liked. We used to love soaking our old bread in that. It was the bread what filled you up, and the juices of the meat and the marrowbones in the gravy what done you good. After breakfast, Mother would put us outside with this big stone jar, full of marrowbones. She thought it was good for us kids to suck 'em. Our tongues would be red raw, but that was beautiful, sucking them bones.

People in the terraced houses always looked really elite on Sundays. The children an' all. Even if we went about a bit untidy during the week, on Sundays we were all dressed up with our clean underwear on. Even the poorest of the poor tried. They polished up their face and took their curlers out. And most of them had shoes on their feet on Sundays. Our shoes were always clean, 'cause the boys used to clean them on the bench outside. Father wore a lovely suit, and his posh cheat, starched and lovely, what Mother had ironed for him. It looked like a shirt and collar. He had studs to put in it, cause it didn't have buttons. That was just a Sunday thing. I don't know if he even had a collar on during the week. But on Sundays his hair was quiffed back, and he wore a trilby and a buttonhole when he went out. A man wouldn't go out on Sunday if he weren't dressed up.

Father was as good as gold on Sundays. He never got drunk and he was a proper gentleman. He used to go off nicely about half past eleven. 'Goodbye Mother,' he'd say, and he'd kiss her. He'd go for a couple of rounds and then he'd come home at the proper time. On the way home, he'd stop at the fruit shop. It was done beautiful. Grapes an' all. He used to buy a pound of Brazil nuts regular, every week. They were for Mother, but we all used to have some. When we saw him coming round the corner, we'd shout: 'Here come Father.' And Mother would get us up to the table, so there wasn't a hubbub like there is with a lot of children. When Father come in, we'd all be up at the table with the best white cloth and our own knife and fork. Sometimes we'd have a bit of beef. Father would cut it all up, and mother would dish it out. The grown-ups would have a fair slice and us kids would have what Mother called 'a taster'. We used to have rabbit a lot. Well, she must have had two rabbits with all us lot round the table. She couldn't do no Yorkshire puddings, 'cause the oven weren't big enough. But she cooked dumplings on top of the cauliflower and cabbage. Oh, they were delicious. They used to float like big balls in the big iron saucepan. We had suet dumplings sometimes, but these Norfolk dumplings were so light. Just flour and water really. Your hands have got to be right to make them. And we always had loads of potatoes and lovely gravy what we would sop up. And marrow fat peas. She used to soak them the night before. After Sunday dinner, the girls used to wash up, while Mother sat on an ordinary straight-backed chair. There was only one easy chair and that was Father's.

Sunday School was horrible. Mother used to say: 'Now go to Sunday School and be a good girl.' All the children used to be dressed up beautifully and clean and lovely. We had an assembly first, where we all got together and said prayers. I used to like that, but not the separate classes. I can remember the teacher quite well. She was horrible. She weren't what I'd call a teacher of religion. She never had no religious countenance or anything. Even if you just moved, she'd shout your name. 'Edwards, keep still and listen to what I'm telling you,' she'd say. She wouldn't say Ethel. I still used to go, but I didn't like it, and I didn't like her.

After Sunday dinner, Father used to sit in the chair reading the paper. 'Father, have you finished?' Mother would say. She used to call him Father, and he called her Mother. Never Christian names. He read the paper first, because they only had one pair of glasses. Ordinary tin ones, sixpence out of Woolworths. Sunday tea, we had shrimps or winkles or salmon. Mother used to open a tin of salmon and put it out on the plates. There was hardly any there, but she'd press a plate on top to make it look more. We had a bit of cucumber and a bit of tomato with it and as much bread and marge as we liked. She had five loaves a day, and you'd get a lot of rounds from that. Then we had dried fruit apple rings, what she bought at the shop to to soak. And on Sunday there'd be a big bowl full. We'd have custard with them. Lovely custard. So you can see that it weren't just opening tins, were it? Everything she done was work.

On Sunday nights in the summer, we had the front door open. Mother and Father used to have their chairs out on the doorstep, and we'd be running about. I'd go across to Maudie Coe's sometimes, and her mother and father would be doing the same. And people used to go past and stop for a little chat. One of the boys would go to the Robin Hood with Father's jug. He'd still have his pint, but he never went out on Sunday evenings. They had this snug where the boys used to go. A jug of beer for Father and a bottle of stout for Mother. Then we'd all sit and eat these Brazil nuts what Father had brought home in the morning. And I thought: 'Oh, I'm happy tonight. Father in't going to come home drunk.' That was horrible, really, when you think a little girl had to worry like that. Sunday was my heavenly day when I was a little girl.

5. School Days

Every morning, when we'd eaten breakfast, Mother did our hair. I couldn't stick that. She'd brush it and comb it, and bring it up the two sides with a bow. Sometimes, we had a bit of a Piccadilly[31] at the front. Most little girls in the terraced houses used to have their mothers put their hair in rags at night. They looked so pretty with their ringlets. I used to envy them. Mother never done them for us. I suppose she was too tired. But she did use to make us look nice. We'd all be clean and I had this lovely white pinafore with a frill round. The girls wore coats in winter. Mother would put mine on. Then she'd get a big old scarf, wrap it round my neck and under my arms, and put a big safety pin in it. I had a little fur hat and my brothers had caps. They didn't have overcoats. There weren't many what did, 'cause they couldn't afford them. They had these corduroy things. Like what they still wear now, but with buttons, 'cause there weren't zips then. And, of course, the boys didn't have long trousers when they were little. Just wool socks up to the knee.

I went to school at St Saviour's.[32] There weren't much of that

---

[31] A fringe

[32] School attendance records show that Ethel Eva Edwards attended St Saviour's Infants from 3 June 1918 to 27 July 1921 and then transferred to St Saviour's School for Girls until 21 December 1928. Just before Ethel's arrival at the second school, a report by a school inspector from the Board of Education, noted: 'Previous to Jan. 1920 there was a mixed school in this building. Many of the girls who were admitted when the reconstitution took place proved to be in a deplorably backward state. The social conditions of the district, too, make the work exceptionally difficult. The Headmistress and her staff deserve praise for the undoubted success, which has attended their efforts to provide training in habits of neatness, cleanliness and punctuality and carefulness and to enlist the interest and good will of the parents.'

truanting business at that time of day. Your parents wouldn't let you, for a start. There used to be a man come round and your mother could get into severe trouble if you weren't at school. I remember, one day, Maudie my friend and I we didn't go. I was in her house, and we saw this big man through the pantry window. He come to the door, and we hid. They were very, very hot on you in them days. Of course, if the mothers knew, we'd get a smack. We weren't really truants. I don't know how we got away with it that time, but we did.

When you went out of your house in the morning, you weren't alone. You'd go out of your house and there'd be loads of children walking to school, from here, there and everywhere. Some with boots, some with shoddy shoes, and some of the poor little things from Barrack Street, with no shoes at all. The school would give them shoes, but some of the mothers sold them. So when it were winter, they couldn't go to school.

Mother would never let us eat outside, but you'd see a lot of the kids eating a bit of toast and dripping on the way to school. I remember one of my friends – Dinky her name was – she always had a big round of toast with thick butter. It was beautiful. We'd walk down our road and along Barrack Street past the brewery and the wagons. The wagon men always looked smart, even though they were poor. They wore a cap, and they had these lovely great leather aprons on, and boots with steel on the ends, 'cause if they dropped a bottle on their foot, that'd break their toes. They were big men, burly men, and they always had a ruddy complexion. Of course, they were out in the air all day and, years ago, they were mostly drinking men. The shire horses, I think that's what they called them, they had brass all hanging

A Steward and Patteson brewery dray delivering to the Black Horse in St Giles Street

down. They were magnificent. The men what driv[33] them really used to take care on 'em. Before we left home, Mother would say to us: 'Mind the horses and carts. Don't you go near them!' Of course, we could have gone to the other side of the road, but we didn't. We kept to the brewery side what was really dangerous. There were quite a lot of deaths. These great big horses and carts used to come out and sometimes people ran off the path and got hit by them and fell under their hooves. You wouldn't stand an earthly if you got in their way. You'd be trampled on. You'd die instantly. Oh yes, you didn't get the car accidents in my day, but you got the accidents with the horses.[34]

꿎

[33] drove

[34] From the *Norwich Mercury* during the period of Ethel's childhood it becomes clear that cars were causing an increasing number of accidents in Norwich – often as a result of pedestrians wandering into the road. Whether or not to establish a speed limit in the city was hotly debated. Not only cars and horses were dangerous. Cattle were driven through the streets of Norwich at this time and, in August 1920, a man living in Barrack Street was crushed by a cow that broke away from the cattle market.

Someone used to ring the bell at the start of school – what I always wanted to do, but never did. We had to go to the classroom first, and then the teacher led us into assembly. I used to love that, 'cause I was always into religion. I'd have got top marks if they'd have had marks for that. We used to have a prayer and a hymn, and then we all went back to the classroom. I remember being cold in winter. There was an open fire where the teacher was. So she was there, taking all our heat away wasn't she? And if we wanted a drink of water, we had to put our hand up and go to the old taps in the yard. It weren't very nice.

The teachers were dressed straightforward. No trimmings, but they always looked neat. Their hair weren't fantastic, 'cause there weren't no styles like there are today. But they was well groomed. Miss Andrews, she was a straight-haired lady. Plump, very fat. She weren't bad, but as she was teaching, she used to put her hand up and then bring it down to her mouth. That used to fascinate me. I used to put more attention on that than on what she was teaching. Miss Briggs was very tall, done-up hair, very rigid looking, and Miss Trollop was one of them little ones with bandy legs[35].

The teachers didn't have to be strict, 'cause we knew our place. We knew we couldn't speak out of turn, and we always put our hand up. The teachers had favourites in them days. And they didn't have much time for them what weren't brilliant. If you were bright, you were spoke to more. If you weren't you were stuck at the back. Me, I weren't really bright. I wasn't very attentive, so really I suppose the teachers had their reasons for not liking me. But if they'd have been kind and made it interesting, I would have took notice, 'cause I weren't really a bad child. Some of the children had all their brothers

[35] Legs that bent outward at the knees.

and sisters what were at work and so their mothers had time to do things with them. They would probably read to them and sing. In my own case, my mother was lively, but she didn't have time to give us individual attention.

I hated swimming lessons. The swimming teacher was horrible, and I was absolutely petrified of water. I got in the pool and I just held onto that bar. But the teacher said: 'Come on, do this and do that.' I was crying, but I wouldn't leave go of the bar. I felt a big coward, but it's terrible when you're frightened. The next day at school, she said: 'Edwards even weeps in the water.' The children made fun of me: 'Bla-baby, bla-baby.'

I was never picked for nothing at school. One time, the teacher was looking for a real good voice to sing at St Andrew's hall. That was the time she came round and heard our voices. I remember singing 'Lead us to that Lonely Shore'. I got it just right, and I think I was the only one. I'm not kidding myself. I really did have a beautiful, little sweet voice. But she passed me. Then, when she got in front of the class, she said: 'Well, there's one person here what's got a beautiful voice, and that's Ethel Edwards. But she's not going to St Andrew's because she's not good.' And she said it as though I'd done a murder or something terrible. I suppose it's because I didn't take any interest in the lessons. But she was naughty. She should have said: 'Ethel, I'll send you, but you must behave yourself more. You must pay more attention to the lessons and be a good girl.' But no, she just humiliated me in front of the class. They did that in them days.

I did love cookery and I was good at it. Just the basics, apple pie and that sort of thing. The lady what taught us – she wasn't a teacher –

she was Scottish. She used to do the school dinners. And sometimes I used to stay and help her. I used to wash up for her and things like that. They weren't school dinners like they are now. They were only for the poor kids. They didn't have to pay. That was just a bowl of soup, but I used to love it. She used to put the potatoes and tomatoes through a sieve. No meat, and a big lump of bread with it. My mother made soup, but this soup was really lovely.

I'd try and get out of school any time I could. I'd say: 'Oh, Mother, I don't feel well.' I'd sometimes make myself be sick. I'd put my finger in my throat, which was terrible. 'There's nothing wrong with her,' my sisters used to say. 'You can't see through her, Mother.' I used to lie on the couch and when I heard the school bell ring – you could hear the bell from our house – I'd get up and say: 'Mother, can I have a penny?' And she'd say: 'I thought you weren't feeling very well.' 'Well,' I say: 'I feel better now.' She never seemed to see through me, or whether she did and felt sorry for me, I don't know.

I remember one particular Friday morning, I was on the couch pretending I wasn't well, and Mother was going to Mr Dawson's the butcher. I heard the bell go for my school and I thought: 'Ooh I know what I can do, I'll whitewash the kitchen and save Mother.' She always used to whitewash the kitchen and the steps on a Friday morning. I wasn't very old. I couldn't have been above eight. Well of course she was gone for a little while. She went to the Co-op[36] and got a few

---

[36] The Co-operative Wholesale Society, founded in 1843, had grocery shops throughout the country. The Co-op was a non-profit making society. Each family shopping there had a Co-op membership number that the shop assistant would record at the time of any purchases. The Society would keep a tally of the total payments made by each member and would make a pro-rata share-out of its profits once a year. This was the much-looked-forward-to dividend or 'divvy'.

things, and then she went for her meat. I did it all right, but the mess I made! And I was full of whitewash myself. By the time Mother come home it was nearly dinner time. She put the basket down and she said: 'Oh my God! What am I going to do?' You see she had to cook, 'cause my brothers and sisters used to come home for dinner. And I say: 'Don't worry Mother. I'll do it.' I got a pail of water and I hurried up and done it. (You know if you lay on a couch pretending you're not well, you can sometimes get ill. Once I done it and I was really, really ill for a few days. And that served me right. Perhaps the Lord thought: 'Well she's naughty. If she want to be ill, let her be ill.')

⁙

The chemist knew I could sing, and he told me about a Madame Tessa, (or something like that), who had a troupe. 'She could teach you to dance as well,' he say. Of course, we had to pay. It was about tuppence on a Saturday morning, and Mother had to scrape around for the coppers. I can remember the first day I went in. Madame was a lovely buxom sort and very much a lady. I think she lived in one of the big houses. Most of the other kids there had mothers with money, and they were all dressed lovely. They didn't have many poor children. There was a fat boy there, and Madame said to me 'Go and dance with him.' And I say: 'No, I in't going to dance'. You know, all silly and giggly. But he kept coming up to dance with me. And, in the finish, I relented and did dance with him. How silly you are when you're young. And how shy.

Anyhow, this little troupe was really good. Madame used to put these shows on in different places. And people paid to come in. Of course, the majority were the children's mothers. One particular time, we had this dance and we were supposed to be the moon and the stars.

I was the moon. I had this little dress on, which was black sort of sateen, not satin. It had a big moon in the front and I had a half moon on my head, and nice little black shoes. But I was annoyed about that, 'cause I wanted to be a star. The stars were beautiful. They were in pale blue, sequin stuff, with a big silver star on the front, and a silver star on their head. I weren't very happy and I don't think I danced very good. I think that was the disappointment about being a moon and not a star what made my mind up that I wasn't going to go no more. Why did I do these things? I could have done so many nice things. But I couldn't care less. I was a very silly little girl. I used to get fed up quick. I loved singing, but dancing weren't my scene. I can still remember one of the songs Madame taught me all them years ago. It's a bit sad when you think about it, but a lot of pregnant women and a lot of mothers died in my day.

> Beautiful baby, wonderful girl,
> You are your daddy's wonderful pal.
> Though you are only eleven months old,
> You are more precious than all the world's gold.
> When you grow up, two sweethearts we'll be.
> You'll take the place of your mother for me.
> Beautiful baby, wonderful girl,
> You are your daddy's wonderful pal.

When the children round where I lived had a party, I was always invited. I thought I was asked to all the parties, 'cause they liked me, but that wasn't really the case. As soon as I got there, they said: 'Come on, Ethel, sing.' I remember one party at my friend Maudie's. Her mother's house was bigger than ours. I think they must have had an extra bedroom. Maudie had several brothers and sisters. They slept in beds four at a time. But they had a nice big front room. And when she said that they were having a party and would I come, I said: 'Of course

I will'. It was a lovely party. We were in a big room, and the children were all dressed up. We had bows of ribbon on our hair, and we had pretty dresses. Not that they were expensive, but they were always pretty. There was always sandwiches for tea, and fruit. People in them days, they didn't used to buy a tin of fruit. I don't know whether that was about, or whether that was out of our reach. They used to soak this dried fruit. You know, apricots, apple rings. You didn't have ice-cream, of course not, but you could have lots of jelly and custard and this 'ere dried fruit, which was lovely. And a few sweets. People used to make home-made toffee and coconut ice, rather than buy it. Then there were always games. They'd hide a present and you had to find it. And you used to play Blind Man's Buff, and Musical Chairs. You ran round and nearly broke your neck. And there was Postman's Knock. You had to go outside and pick someone's number. Then they'd come out. It was dark and you had to kiss them.

Our mother didn't have time for parties. She had too many of us at home to feed. The kids who had parties, they were from smaller families, or else they had brothers and sisters what were married. So did I, but there were still so many of us in the house. There was twelve at home when I was born, as well as Mother and Father. And they were there for years. They weren't married young. They wouldn't be allowed, unless something happened. And it didn't, I'm pleased to say.

⊰▣⊱

The street was our playground when we were little. Kids didn't used to sit in much, even in winter. We'd just put a scarf on and go out. We couldn't play with our friends indoors, because there was too many of us already. We'd go in for food from time to time, but then we'd go out and play again. I remember once I was playing with my little friend

Mabel in her mother's garden. We found an old tin bath out there. I don't know what it was doing outside. Maybe they'd had a bath the night before. There weren't room in the house for big baths. That's why our mother used to hang ours on the inside of the coal shed door. We were playing ever so nice that day, and I said: 'I'm going to get in the bath.' I must have been very tiny. I stripped and she stripped and we got into this bath. Mother was working inside the house at the time. She didn't think of seeing two kids naked in the bath, did she? Someone must have told her in the end, 'cause I remember her coming with a blanket and coming and picking me up. 'Oh you naughty girl,' she said. And she wrapped me up, took me indoors, put me near the fire and dressed me.

One day I went out in the street and there was two or three girls. I said: 'I'm going to have a party today. I'll be the princess. And if you can get a penny each, you can come.' We went across to Mrs Howlett's and got a hap'orth[37] of turnip, a hap'orth of carrots, and a hap'orth of sweets. I cut them all up. Then I got my blackboard, put it over the lavatory seat, and we had a party in the lavatory. Other times, I used to like pretending I was a rich lady. An old bit of curtain what Mother had finished with, I'd put that round me. If there was any old beads about, I'd thread 'em up, all different shapes and sizes and colours. And then I'd put a bit of cotton round my ear and have a couple of beads hanging down. My sisters had a shelf up the corner of our room, where they had cosmetics and I used to get up there and make up. A cheap face powder called Tishaniang, or something like that, what came in a yellow and orange box with flowers on. And a

---

[37] A halfpenny worth

lovely box of powder with all little powder puffs. Then I'd put my own shoes on inside my sisters' shoes. They were their best shoes, and if they knew that, they would have killed me. But I was a bit clever as a kid. If I done it, I made sure I weren't leaving any traces. And then I used to lay on the old couch 'smoking' – a bit of white paper in a piece of cardboard, like one of them holders what the rich ladies used. I used to think I was the cat's whiskers with all this on.

'I've got a piano now,' I said to my friends one time. 'You haven't,' they say, and they were right. We never had a piano. But we got this 'ere tin trunk and I tried to make out that it was a piano. 'You can hear it,' I said. I went in the house and banged on the trunk and I think I convinced them that I had one. I was happy, 'cause you know if you had a piano, it meant you were ever so rich. One day my friend Maudie said: 'We've got a piano now.' She didn't really want it. Why couldn't I have had it, 'cause I really did want one. 'Can I come in your front room and play your piano?' I say: 'Ask your mother if I can.' We went in her front room and there it was. That weren't a modern one, but that was a nice one. Of course, I couldn't play the piano, but I must have played a good tune up, 'cause her mother come through and she say: 'Play that again.'

We had a big skipping rope what went right across the road. It was the rope what come from the orange boxes. Years ago, when the shops used to have oranges, they come in a wooden case. A lot of people used to put a cloth over the top and have them for a bit of furniture. The rope what come round the cases was more like a braided rope. That was quite heavy really. We'd take a turn of turning it when we played skipping. Other times we tied it on the lamp-post at the corner of our road. The one what the man used to come and light. It was a big iron lamp post and it was steady at the bottom. We got a bigger girl to climb up and tie the rope on near the top. There was a ridge which it held on and made it secure. You then used to run round the lamp post and lift your feet off the ground and swing round on the rope. You'd go round and round and you'd be all right, but then suddenly you'd go wrong and you'd twizzle and turn all the way round and bump your head. And when it came to a halt, you'd often bang your head again. Ooh it'd be terrible, but it didn't put us off.

I used to like marbles. I don't think we ever made a hole ourselves. Well, we couldn't have done, 'cause that was all concrete. But there's always a little hole in the pavement isn't there? We'd play marbles, but mine never went in. When we'd finished, our little finger was filthy dirty, but we didn't care. We didn't go in to wash. We didn't keep going indoors to wash like they do today. I think that's why we were more healthy, 'cause we lived amongst the dirt.[38] 'Buttons' was a bit like marbles. We drew a circle with a lump of chalk. Not chalk like they have on the board; that were a ha'penny a box and we couldn't afford it. We used to get it from a chalk hill on the heath. You had to try and get your button in the circle. When it went in, you kept it. When it didn't go in the ring, you lost it. Irene, my little friend, she used to get them in every time. She had a big box of buttons. But I never could win. I used to go out with my few buttons, and Irene would take the lot. I think I was in too much of a hurry. I threw either too soft so they didn't go in, or so hard, that when I got them in the ring, they'd then fly out and I'd go home crying for more. Mother used

---

[38] It is interesting that, eighty years on, some researchers would agree with Ethel's supposition. There is growing concern that children may be more susceptible to allergies and weakened immune systems because they are exposed to fewer bacteria.

to say: 'Oh, you craze me.' But she'd open up the shed and cut some buttons off the coats. I think they were coats my brothers brought back from the war. She kept them for when she patched the boys' trousers, and to put on the bed when it was really cold.

We used to play whip and top. We'd get different coloured chalk and make the top orange or green. The whip was just a little bit of stick with a bit of string on. We'd whip the top and sometimes we could keep it up for a long time. Some were clever at it and kept their top going all morning. We didn't get bored. We used to love it.

⊰⊱

Every Sunday there was a band on the parks. We had some really good summers in them days[39]. You might have got an odd thunder storm, 'cause I remember standing on the stool and looking out the window at the rain beating on the ground. Mother used to say: 'Come and look at the dancing dollies.' 'Cause that's what it looked like.

In the holidays the kids would go up Mousehold.[40] It was just near us. We'd go about nine o'clock in the morning and come home at tea time. We always took something to eat and drink. Mother, used to make up a big jug of that lemonade what was in powder form, and pour it in a bottle for us. Sometimes, if she had a ha'penny we'd go to

---

[39] Ethel is not alone in remembering long hot summers of childhood. In fact, a look at meteorological data for the 1920s shows that the number of dry sunny days in Norwich was not much different from the average of seven decades later.

[40] Mousehold Heath is a short walk from where Ethel lived. It covers 184 acres and is all that remains of a much larger open space used by local villagers, centuries before, as common land for their sheep and cows. It was on Mousehold Heath in 1549 that people's hero, Robert Kett, gathered a band of about 16,000 peasants in rebellion against the landowners. During the 19th century, the heath was quite a wild place and was much frequented by the English Roma who knew it as 'Harisky Tan' or the heath of the graves. In 1886, what was left of Mousehold Heath was declared by the Mayor to be a recreation ground for ever – thus saving it from developers.

The Bandstand on Mousehold Heath

Mrs Goodson's house and we'd get a ha'penny bottle of Oreround[41].
She used to make it herself. That was like the root beer they have
today. Similar, but nicer. She was a big plump lady, clean and nice, no
teeth. Well, I think she had one big tooth at the side. Sometimes we
had corned beef sandwiches. That was cheap, tuppence a quarter. Or
we'd have bread and dripping or bread and cheese. A couple of loaves
Mother used to do, but then she got rid of us all for a whole day didn't
she?

We used to go up the big sandhill on Mousehold to what we called
the 'mussel ranger's house'.[42] I don't know why they say the 'mussel
ranger's', but that's what we called it. It was on the top of a hill, a

[41]This drink, which Ethel found so delicious, was no doubt made from white hore
hound, a plant of the mint family that Mrs Goodson grew or gathered locally. A syrup
made from hore hound was used to ease bronchitis and other respiratory problems.

[42] A full-time ranger lived on and looked after the heath. 'Mussel' is a contraction of
Mousehold.

lovely big house with a porch and a brick wall round it. The caretaker of Mousehold lived there. We used to play shops on the sandhill. We imagined everything. We imagined people coming in the shop, imagined they wanted to put some money on the book. We used to pretend that the sand was sugar and then put it in old paper bags. One time I found some glass in the sand, and I think, oh, toffee. I'll break it up and put it in bags. I got a great bit of stone and hit it. But I didn't cut my hand. How did I not cut my hand? Perhaps the Lord thought: 'Bless her heart. She don't know. I'll not let anything happen to her.'

⁂

I can't remember this happening, 'cause I weren't born. But one day, Mother said to my sisters, Hilda, Edie, Rosy and Clara: 'For goodness sake, all you lot go upstairs and play till I get this job done.' Well, my sister told me they were all playing lovely upstairs. My brother Sam was up there as well, and they were playing in our second bedroom. Then, Sam wanted to wee. That meant he had to come downstairs and go outside, 'cause there was no toilet inside. So he must have thought: 'I'll just wee out of this window.' So, he just stood there, weeing. Hilda caught him doing it and she was so mad that she pushed him out of the window. There were sash windows and you can fall out easy when they're pulled up high. Fortunately, Sam managed to catch hold of the washing line as he fell and then he was able to swing over to the bench and jump off. If the line hadn't been there, he would have been killed 'cause there was all the steps underneath. But he didn't have a bone broken. Mother was busy in the kitchen and when she saw him walk in the door she nearly had a fit. Hilda got a good hiding, 'cause that was a serious thing, pushing people out of windows. She couldn't have been that old, 'cause if you were older you wouldn't push anyone out of the window. Some people used to take the line in, but not Mother. She was two days washing and ironing, and she didn't have no time for bringing lines in and putting them out.

Every year we had an outing on the coal cart. I think that was a poor children's outing for the children of our district. Them what were a bit better off didn't want to go on a coal cart did they? But I always went. Weren't that good of these coal men? Giving up their day and their horses, 'cause that was their livelihood. There'd be two or three carts full. We didn't have no forms to sit on. But they used to sweep the carts out and then put clean sacks in. I know we never got dirty, so they must have cleaned them really well. There'd be about twenty of us kids on a coal cart, all sitting with our legs folded. We used to go to Whitlingham,[43] because you could go by the side of the river there. There was this big shed, and there was these trestle tables inside. No chairs. And all these plates of strawberries with sugar. A whole plate of strawberries on your own. Mother sometimes used to give us three or four with a big bit of bread and butter, but that was all. Cor, we got stuck into them and we didn't half enjoy ourselves. We sat by the river and watched the swans. We played ball. We played 'Poor Mary Is A Weeping', 'The Farmer's In The Den', 'Ring A Ring O' Roses', 'Ding Dong Bell', and 'Oranges and Lemons'. That was wonderful.

Once a year, the men what went to the Robin Hood,[44] they'd have an outing. Sometimes they had a fishing outing when they fished. A

---

[43] Whitlingham is on the banks of the river on the outskirts of Norwich. Now a country park, it is still a popular location for picnics and recreation.

[44] i.e. the regular drinkers at the Robin Hood public house.

big wagon and two big shire horses used to come for 'em early in the morning. Half would have a tie on, but the other half wouldn't. And it must have been about nine o'clock when they got back home. It was exciting for all us kids. We used to ask our mothers if we could keep up. When they got back, they'd get out of the wagon and go in the Robin Hood. But the man who'd driven them used to give us a little ride round before he went in. I suppose he thought: 'It's better for me to give the kids a ride than have them jumping in and upsetting the horses when I'm in the pub'. He give us a little ride up the road and back, and then we had to get out. But we were satisfied and we all went home to our house.

⋅⊰⊱⋅

Wednesday nights were wonderful for me, because Mother and I used to go to the pictures.[45] Sometime I used to take friends. I'd say: 'Do you want to come to the pictures with my mother?' And we all used to go together. My sisters would say: 'Carting a lot of kids! Mother don't want that.' But I was like that. Mostly though, it was just Mother and me. I used to get hold of her arm, and on the way, we'd stop and buy a quarter of sweets for tuppence. Mother would have her big hat on, but as soon as we got in the pictures, she'd turn round to the people behind, and say: 'Ooh my dears, can you see?' And she'd take her hat off. It were a silent picture, so there were subtitles. But there was lots

---

[45] The Cinema came to Norwich in 1911 just three years before Ethel's birth with the opening of the Picture House in 1911 in Haymarket in the city centre. Admissions from 6d to 1/-. The first purpose-built cinema was Cinema Palace in Magdalen Street in 1912 with 850 seats. Behaviour in cinemas was often quite rough and it was quite common for children to throw things at each other, particularly between the stalls and the circle. In this cinema in February 1920, William Watson of Mousehold Street (a near neighbour of Ethel) struck an attendant in an argument over blocking the gangway. He was brought before the Court and fined 5/-.

of people couldn't read. So all round the theatre, you could hear different people reading what was written on the screen out loud. Like 'I love you' and all that. And not all at the same time. One was saying this and one was saying that. When we'd finished, it'd be about nine o'clock. We'd go home and Mother would say: 'Shall we go to bed?', 'cause she was always tired. I used to love getting in her big feather bed. If it was cold, she'd say: 'Breathe down the bed.' And we used to both breathe down the bed, and I'd snuggle near her. When my dad come home, he'd come in and he'd carry me off to bed. He wouldn't wake me up.

One night, we were going to the pictures and I said: 'Mother, can we have some Brazil nuts instead of sweets?' Well, we sat in the pictures, and mother bit into a nut and broke her tooth. She shouldn't really have been cracking 'em with her false teeth. I was upset about it. I thought, ooh poor Mother got to pay to have it repaired. We forgot about it while we were at the pictures. But the next day, when my older sisters realised she'd

The Haymarket Picture House

got her tooth broken, I got told off. 'If that weren't for you, Mother wouldn't have her tooth broken. She didn't want the Brazil nuts. It's you what wanted them.' I were really hurt and worried. I thought it was my fault. I shouldn't have asked for Brazil nuts. I wish I'd just asked for sweets. Poor Mother had to save up quite a bit to have a new tooth put in. I think it was five shillings to go to the dentist, but she was very particular about her appearance.

On Saturday mornings, Mother used to give us a few coppers for the pictures.[46] It was a penny and we had to sit two on a seat. I had to sit with my big fat brother, Frank. Nobody else wouldn't sit with him, 'cause he took up nearly the whole seat. I didn't mind, 'cause I liked to be with my Franky. He was ever so kind and loving. He used to take me on his shoulders and walk with me. He was really a lovely boy. But in that day when you were fat or anything, the kids would laugh at you. I remember being on his back one time, and walking past Riverside. Someone shouted: 'Eh boy, does your mother starve you?' And I shouted: 'No, she don't starve him. He have lots of food.' Of course, they meant it sarcastic because he was so fat, but I couldn't see it that way. It broke my heart. If I'd have got down from his shoulders, I think I would have kicked him what shouted. Frank was always fat, and I think he was shy. He never went with girls. He was a nice-looking boy, but he was fat.

Before the picture started, the kids used to throw stuff at each other. Oh that was a riot. Then, when this lady come, a short fat little lady, busking down the aisle, they used to throw bits of carrot at her. Poor woman. She played an introduction and then she would make all the noises with the piano. They were clever in them days, because they

---

[46] On Saturday mornings, the cinemas used to screen films for children.

did do it right. They really tuned in with the film. Charlie Chaplin, Buster Keaton, Mary Pickford were on, and of course, Laurel and Hardy. We used to love them, because they were so funny. And Lillian Gish, we used to see her on Saturday mornings. One week, someone got her and tied her to the railway line, and the train was coming towards her. We were all off our seats and standing up. 'Look out! Look out!' We were all screaming. Then, when the train nearly got to her, it said 'Continued next week'. And the next Saturday, a chap would come by on a lovely big horse and whip her off the rails. Or the train would go on another rail or something. We were all relieved. But then at the end of that episode there was something similar. At the Electric Cinema, (I think that was in Oak Street) you could get in without paying if you took a rabbit skin or a jam jar.

Sometimes Mother would say: 'We'll all go to the Hippodrome[47] tonight.' Cor, we were excited all day at school. Mother wore her black coat and black hat with a brim. I don't remember Father coming. There was always big queues. I used to love it when you stood in the queue, 'cause people would come along selling things before you went in. An old gentleman, whose wife had a cardboard nose, used to come with his big tray. He had magazines on it, and almanacs. And he'd sell peanuts. Then another man would be selling oranges. They didn't have usherettes with ice creams like they do today. When they opened the doors, we charged up to the gods[48] like hooligans. That was the

---

[47] The Hippodrome was the home of the Music Hall and variety shows in Norwich for many years. It was an imposing building opened in 1903 and first known as The Grand Opera House. It was demolished in 1966 to make way for the St Giles Street multi-storey car park.

[48] The seats that were the highest up (closest to 'the gods') in the theatre.

only place we could afford. We used to run up and get at the front. There was a lovely balcony, so if you could get seats round there you were well away. Poor Mother. She couldn't get up there quickly like us kids. But she used to get there in the end, bless her heart.

The Hippodrome, St Giles' Street, Norwich

There were comics, and a pianist and a man on a violin. And you'd see a couple of acrobats. Nothing out of the ordinary, but I remember once, they had a boxing ring and there was two ladies boxing. It wasn't a real boxing match. That was only fun, but my heart was a beating. I thought, oh they're going to hurt each other. We saw real violence up the yards and in the streets all the time and we accepted that. But to go to the theatre and see two women boxing, I was frightened out of my life. Then we used to have a lady come on that sing the old time music hall songs. These were always buxom ladies and they all had big boobs. And there were dancers, them with frilly things, cocking their legs up and showing their knickers.

6. Friends and Neighbours

Maudie and me, we were really good old pals. She lived across the road from us in a biggish house, with a great big front room. There was quite a family live there: a sister, with her husband and two children, and then two brothers and another sister. Her mother used to work for a doctor. Short she was, a hunched-up little woman. And she used to wear a little cap. Maudie was like me. Her mother had her late in life. Her father was an old man. Well, they were all old people in them days, even young people. He was very quiet and pale, a tall man with a moustache. He didn't go out to work. He mended boots and shoes in his shed, heeling shoes and soling them. In my day, people had that done all the time, so in the finish the uppers wore out before the soles. Poor old boy. It wasn't much of a job and you can bet he didn't get much.

There were stairs up the middle of Maudie's house. And that's where we saw the ghost. Suddenly, one of the kids said: 'There's a ghost up the stairs.' So we all dared one another to run up to see if the ghost was still there. There we were, running up and down the stairs, screaming. And everyone say they saw this ghost. Well, of course, there weren't no such thing as a ghost. What naughty children, running up and down this lady's stairs, screaming and shouting. Must have been terrible, but nobody was there to tell us off. Her mother and father were at the Robin Hood. That's where most people were on a Saturday evening.

There was a little girl lived opposite me. Her name was Irene. There weren't too many in the family. Just two sisters and a brother.

Her mother had her on the change.[49] I suppose she was in her early 50s, but in them days the women always looked elderly. She had rolled-up sleeves and an apron on, and her hair twisted on the top. I used to walk home from school with Irene, and I remember her mother always had a cup of milk for her. Hot milk. She used to come out the door with it. 'Come on, Irene, drink this milk.' But Irene didn't want it. She used to have a couple of sips and put the rest down the drain. She was a good mother, but she was a silly woman really. She ought to have made sure Irene drank it. It's a wonder she didn't notice it. Milk don't all go down the drain, do it. I used to think: 'Give it to me. I'll drink it all up for you.' It was all cups of weak tea for us. The brothers and sisters what were grown up, they used to have a nice cup of tea. But we used to have ours in a big jug, sweet and watery. Mother wouldn't have been able to give us a cup of milk each. I don't know why Irene didn't let me drink hers, but she never did.

Then there was my friend Tilly Cadge. She had really blonde hair and a roughish voice. I think her mother had her on the change, but she was perfectly alright. She didn't get this post-natal thing. Tilly was a little tear-away, but she was a nice little girl, and she used to come round mine to play. Now, one of my sisters had a lovely watch. That was a gold one with all blue round the edge. Well, after Tilly had gone one day, I missed this watch. And I thought, oooh dear. I mean I weren't really responsible, because who'd have thought she would have took it, but I knew she was the only one there. It probably fascinated her and you can bet she thought: 'I'll have that.' Well, I was worried to death. I thought, ooh, when my sister come home and find her watch

---

[49] During the menopause

gone I'll be in trouble. It was very traumatic for me, because though we were a big family and poor, we would never even dream of touching someone else's things. I went over to Tilly's house. 'Tilly,' I said, 'did you borrow my sister's watch?' I had to be really diplomatic. She had it on her ankle, and I really had to wheedle it out of her. I could have went over there and started telling her off, but then her mother would have hit her, 'cause in them days, if they did anything like that, their mother and father beat them up.

Old Mrs Barker lived next door. She was ever such a peculiar woman. She was dark and little, put you in mind of a Gypsy to look at, but I don't think she was. Lolly was her only girl and I remember Mrs Barker ill-treating her quite a bit. When Lolly was a young woman, she used to go out, and if she came home a bit late, her mother would beat her. I've heard my mother say: 'That old bitch is hitting her again.' Of course, you couldn't do nothing about it at that time of day. You couldn't go to the police. They wouldn't want to know. If people wanted to beat their kids, or strap 'em, they done it. They could beat 'em to death if they wanted to. Well, more or less.[50]

When the old girl died, Lolly went to live with someone else. And some relatives of theirs moved into the house. They were nice people. Nicky, the daughter was my friend, but her mother had a baby on the change and she went funny. I felt sorry for Nicky, so one day I took her mother round to mine for a little while. Her nails were all black.

---

[50] There is an ongoing debate as to whether people are less safe now than they were a generation or so in the past. During the period of Ethel's childhood, there were certainly many instances of domestic violence, child abuse and rape and most went unreported to the police. People of that day would have found it difficult to believe that MPs could discuss, as they did in 2004, whether to make smacking an offence.

Whether it was blood I don't know, but my mother said to me: 'Look at her nails. She don't wash her hands.' Poor woman. The father kept her there for some years, but in the finish she had to go away to the asylum. She wasn't very old, but she must have got so she couldn't look after the children.

My friend Hannah had ginger hair. She'd always be getting me to sing. She was a lot older than me, but she thought I was lovely, and that I could sing beautiful. She used to invite me to sing when they had a party. Her father was a fisherman and he had a great big gold earring. That was unusual for most men in that day, but fishermen did have an earring in one ear for some reason. I think that was a bit superstitious. He was always away fishing in the night, so sometimes Hannah used to invite me to sleep at hers. They had this beautiful, big feather bed and there'd be Hannah sleeping in it, and her mother sleeping in it, and me sleeping in it. Sometimes I used to read to the mother, 'cause she couldn't read. It was a paper, the *Red Letter* that was called, and I read from page to page. And Hannah used to come in and she'd say: 'You're reading the wrong'un Ethel. You got to continue on another page when it tells you to. So, I was running all the stories into one. I wasn't learned enough to take that in.

Later on, Hannah had a baby out of wedlock, which was quite rare for a girl in my day. For a start they couldn't afford to, 'cause there was no help whatever. And when it did happen, it was severely looked down on. But I'll tell you one thing. There were a lot of girls what got pregnant, but they got married straight away before you even knew it.[51] Even if the boy didn't know the girl, her parents expected him to

[51] See the footnote on page 7.

marry her. I only remember two girls what had babies out of wedlock. Hannah, and a woman what lived the opposite side of Cavalry Street. She was a haughty young woman and very strait-laced. She just had a mother and father, and a sister and brother. We never dreamed she would ever be in that position, because the whole family was so proud. They looked down on such as my family. They weren't really posh, but they thought they were. They really did think they were the cat's whiskers. She was a person you'd never even think would go with a man, let alone have a baby. She didn't look nothing. It must have been a shock for her parents, 'cause she had twins. We all accepted it, but behind her back we were saying: 'Oh, fancy her doing that! She thought she was better than everyone else, but now we're better than her.' As soon as she had the babies, she had to go back to work. But you've got to hand it to her mother. She kept them two twins and she brought them up beautifully. I don't know what happened to the girl, but I don't think she ever married.

I had a lot of nice friends, but I had some nasty ones as well. They used to have nice clothes, and they used to have money. When I say money, I mean, they had more than what we had. Their mothers probably had two or three children instead of seventeen like my mother. And they were a little bit nose-up-in-the-air. You weren't really as good as them. Well, according to them you weren't. Two or three times a week, they'd get a ha'penny to spend. I remember one time, I fell out with one of them. And if you fell out with one, they'd all fall out with you. There was about five or six of them. They were horrible to me. They kept laughing at me, and screaming out. And that's very degrading. Then all of a sudden, one of them come up to me and she said: 'Ethel, do you want to play with us?' I said: 'Yes please.' And she said: 'Well, we don't want to play with you.' I cried. I went indoors and cried. Mother said: 'Don't pay attention to them. They're no good, if they're like that. You don't need friends like that.' She gave me a ha'penny, and I went and bought a hap'orth of sweets. Yes, the kids who were better off could be nasty. They used to say: 'Oh, she stinks.' But I can swear that we never smelt, 'cause Mother used to bath us and we always had the carbolic soap what took the smell away. Of course, there was some little children what smelt. Like I said, they had a job to keep clean. But how them kids could be nasty like that, I don't know.

7. Living on the Edge

People used to borrow from each other in them days. It was a way of life. You'd see them walking along the street with a cup of sugar or flour in their hand. But then they'd bring it back the next day, or when they got paid. Most people borrowed off Mr Carver, Mother an' all. At Christmas time they'd borrow a fiver from him, 'cause they had to buy presents didn't they? Then in the summer, they used to go and borrow again so they could go down Yarmouth when the holiday come around. They couldn't save up five pounds, but they could afford a few shillings a week. Of course, they had to pay an extra shilling or two for borrowing it, so you know Mr Carver done alright. He was a short little man in a bowler hat and a pin-striped suit. And he always had a nice tie and shiny shoes. When I was a little girl, he used to come every Saturday for his money. My brothers and sisters what were married would bring their money down on Friday night, so mother had it all ready for him. They had a card each and they always paid. The minute we saw him on the street, one of us would run in and say: 'Mr Carver's now coming.' I can see him now, in his horn-rimmed glasses, sitting at the table with all the cards. Then off he went, and the next week he'd come again. His daughter had a shop in Magdalen Street. That was a sweet shop and a fruit shop and if you didn't want anyone to know you were borrowing, you could go there. You could walk through to a room at the back and people didn't know what you was doing.

Mother never went to the pawnshop, but there were loads of women what did. Even in the terraced houses a lot of them done that.

You'd see them marching down the street on a Monday morning with their parcels. I don't think most men knew the wives pawned their suits, because during the week they wore old jackets and old trousers, and wrappers round their necks. And directly they got their money on Friday nights, the women would get the suits out of the pawn shop. Every self-respecting man had a suit that he wore on Sunday, one suit that was a good suit and could last a lifetime. One time, there was a man had to go to a funeral in the middle of the week, but his wife had put his suit in the pawn shop,[52] and they didn't have the money to get it out. There was a big fight, and you can bet your life that he gave her a good hiding.

There weren't many in Cavalry Street what didn't have a little book.[53] Mother would start off every Monday with hers. She'd go into Mrs Howlett's and buy some sugar, marge, or whatever, and Mrs Howlett would write it down in the book. You didn't get a big order like you do now. That was day to day. Tuesday perhaps she'd miss, but then she'd go in Wednesday and buy several things. If you went in for just one thing, like some pickled onions, Mrs Howlett would put pickled onions down in the book, but if you went in for a pound of

[52] Pawnshops were often at their busiest on a Monday morning as women would bring in their husband's Sunday suits. The money they received for them would be used to buy food and essentials until the next pay packet arrived on Friday. The suit would then be redeemed for a price somewhat higher than the money paid out for it. The effective interest rate on the money that this represented was generally lower than that available from money lenders. Pawnshops were the most common providers of short-term credit to poor people. Unemployed families would often pawn all their items of value before submitting themselves to the humiliation of the means test. The number of shops began falling from the late 1930s onwards as the living standards of the poor began to rise.

[53] A small note book in which the shopkeeper recorded the goods taken on credit, and the date they were paid for.

sugar, some marge, some lard, some tea, she'd just put 'goods', and Mother didn't like that. She might have bought ten things, but all it said was 'goods'. Sometimes we went for Mother. I've never known her borrow, so if she ran short of one or two things, she'd send one of us to Mrs Howlett's. We'd run over and when we bring the stuff back, she'd look at the book, and say: 'Now what has she put 'goods' down for? Why doesn't she put down what I've had?' She wouldn't tell Mrs Howlett she didn't like it, 'cause you didn't do that in them times. But that annoyed her and it worried her. She'd keep going over her book. 'That woman, she's a robbin' me,' she used to say. And you can bet Mrs. Howlett done that. The shopkeepers in that day, they did diddle people. Put a little extra on each thing, because they had to make a little money themselves. Mother used to say: 'When I can get out of her clutches, I will. Then I'll get to the Co-op[54] and pay my way.' But you see, once she'd squared her bill up Friday for the week, she didn't have a penny left. I don't know how Mother managed to clear that debt up, but she did square up Mrs Howlett in the end. I don't know if she borrowed something off Mr Carver, or if she come by a shilling or two. But if we ever went to Mrs Howlett's after that, that would be for something what she forgot, or for a couple o' penn'orth of pickled onions what she got the money for.

Mother could make a little money go a long way, but when she got really stuck, there was the little red pillar box[55] on the end of the mantelpiece. The older ones used to put a penny in it when they come

---

[54] See the footnote on p.51.

[55] Money boxes were often in the form of Royal Mail pillar boxes. Money would be 'posted' through the slot in the same way as letters.

round on a Saturday night. That was to buy all the beer and nuts for Christmas, wasn't it? 'Cause they all used to come to ours at Christmas. I don't know why they nailed it down, I expect they wanted it to be safe. But why? No one would steal it. Can you imagine anyone going to all that trouble for a few coppers? From time to time, Mother would borrow four or five pence from the box. She say: 'I'll put that back when one o'em give me a little money.' It was easy putting the pennies in, but hard to get them out. She used to get a knife and push it in and draw the coppers out that way. Well, one time just before Christmas, my brother-up-the-road say: 'We'd better get that box off the mantelpiece.' So they ripped it off and they were a lot short. Mother must have took more money than she should. She cried and she said: 'Wait till I get Mr Carver's money. Then I'll pay it back.' Poor old thing. You can bet she hadn't spent any of it on herself.

❧

When my brother Robert died, Mother didn't have money for the funeral. I wasn't born, but I've heard the story. One day he had convulsions, and died. Mother cried and cried: 'I can't put my baby in a cardboard box.' Can you imagine loving your baby, cuddling it and feeding it, and then just putting it in a cardboard box in the ground? So Mother said to my sister: 'We're going up to see that old devil.' That's what she used to call her brother. She hated to go and crawl and beg to him, but she wasn't having her baby in a cardboard box, 'cause that wasn't no proper burial. She pleaded with Uncle Billy on her knees. 'I'm not going out of this house until you give me a guinea,'[56] she cried. He said no at first, but he gave it her at the finish

---

[56] A guinea was twenty one shillings.

and she got the baby buried nicely. It's terrible when you think of it. There must have been lots of people who put their babies in cardboard boxes. I bet they weren't even buried in a cemetery, because you had to pay for the service and to have the ground taken up.

Even though Mother never had much money, we always had good shoes. There was this man what worked at Southall's[57] shoe factory and he used to get all these seconds. I forget his name now, but we used to go to his house. They had a lot of children. I can remember two babies sitting in a pram with no wheels on. It were a bit like a boat. I suppose they just took the wheels off, and used it like a high chair. I don't think they had baby chairs in them days. If they did, most people couldn't afford them. One time when we went, I got a brown pair of shoes. One was dark brown and one was light. Another time, I had two left feet. They were brown calf shoes with brown laces. I couldn't walk properly, so I had to tell them at school that I was crippled in one foot. It was a white lie, but I wouldn't dare tell them I had two odd shoes on. You know what kids are like in the playground. I didn't want them saying: 'Oh, she got two left shoes.' The whole school would have heard about it, and they'd have laughed. I don't know whether it damaged my foot or not. It must have done a bit, I suppose. But there you are. Mother did the best she could for us.

⌐⊫

It was one and six to have your chimney swup[58] in them days. And that was a lot of money. So, one day in the school holidays, Mother would say to us: 'You've got to stay at home today. Ethel, you stay

[57] After the Second World War, Southall's became Startrite shoes.

[58] swept

with me. Charlie, you watch if a policeman come and Nelly you go with him.' In them days there were always a bobby[59] on the beat and setting fire to a chimney is like setting light to a house, isn't it? You'd have got fined. Mother used to get this newspaper soaked in paraffin and push it up the chimney with a broom. She then set fire to it, and you could hear it roar. She had to do it on a windy day, so that it roared up. 'It's coming through,' yelled Charlie. Flames, smoke, and red hot lumps of soot. And then it used to come down quick. Red hot, great lumps of soot as big as your hand, pouring down into the fireplace. Everything, the mat and the pictures, the mantelpiece fringe, they'd all had to come down. And then there'd be a big spring clean. Hard work it were, cleaning it all up. Charlie stayed around for about three hours. He'd come in and go out again. He had to keep going out to look, just in case the chimney caught fire. Luckily it never did. But fancy Mother doing that. Poor old girl.

⊰⧓⊱

People in my day made money out of everything. They had to. The rag-and-bone-man'd come round the streets.[60] I don't know what rags he got. The people were wearing rags themselves. Mother sometimes had an old coat on the door for him, or she might have a couple of rabbit skins. She used to cut round the eyes with a little sharp knife.

---

[59] policeman

[60] A rag and bone man was the recycler of his day. He would take his horse and cart round the streets collecting any items that were of no use to a household but which he could sell as scrap. He would pay for what he received, often with clothes pegs or balloons or trinkets for children. He would then sell on what he collected for recycling; old rags could be converted into fabric or paper, rabbit skins into clothes or hats, and bones into glue. The rag and bone man would shout out 'Rag and Bone!' or 'Any old iron?' as he walked the streets. His shouts were easily recognized but rarely intelligible – 'any old iron?' generally became 'e ol' eye-n'.

And then she'd hang them up in the coal shed to dry out. She'd get a few coppers from the rag and bone man or we'd go and sell them at the second hand shop for tuppence.

By the time I was born, life was a bit easier for Mother because my older brothers and sisters were earning, but one Friday evening, my brother Billy didn't come home after work. 'Where's Billy?' asked Mother. He didn't come home for his tea, nor that night, nor the next and Mother was frantic. She never thought of going to the police, 'cause you didn't go to the police for them sort of things in them days. But Father rooted around, and found this ginger-haired man with a big moustache. Poor, very poor, and very rough. 'Who you looking for?' he say to Father. 'I'm trying to find my son,' Father said. The vagabond, he say he knew where Billy was. So he come back to the house with Father. Mother said to him: 'I haven't got any money, but if you're hungry, I can give you some food.' She gave him a big plate, bread all piled up, cheese, and a hot cuppa cocoa. And he told Father that Billy was in a place for down-and-outs in Bank Plain. Of course, Father went and got him. I can remember them coming through the door. Billy were crying. Mother said: 'Oh my boy, why did you do it?' And he said it was because he had been given his cards[61] and he wouldn't be able to pay his board. 'We've got enough for you,' Mother said. I can see him now, going to the sink sobbing, and stripping to his waist. He must have been in that place two or three days, and he felt dirty. He washed his face and his head and all over. That was the first thing he did, rather then went to the pub. Billy was our lovely boy, the one what was thinking of Mother, bless his heart.

[61] Sacked from his job.

A few weeks later, we were together, my married brothers and sisters an' all and I say: 'Oooh, what about when our Billy done a bunk?'[62] Well everyone went quiet. Poor Billy he didn't know where to look and I thought: 'What have I done? What have I said?' They all looked at me daggers. You know you're so innocent when you're small and things come out. That's why I say children never tell lies. They're very honest little children, aren't they? So that was that.

⊰⊱

I don't remember sister Edie getting married to Arthur, but she told me that a week before she got married he got the sack. In them days, you didn't get no money at first. Then it was just a few shillings, and you were only allowed that for so many weeks. At the end of them weeks if you hadn't got a job, you just didn't get no money. Edie had a job at Colman's,[63] but they sacked you when you got married. Arthur said: 'Well what you going to do? Do you want to call it off?' She said: 'Oh no! Let's get married. We got the house.' That was a little two-roomed house, in St Augustine's Way. One up and one down and no water. I think Mother must have helped them. As much as we wanted food ourselves, she always found money to spare if the girls or boys wanted anything. They got over them first two weeks, but Edie didn't get another job for years, 'cause she didn't know no trade. Later on, when I was working, I got her into the boot work. She didn't

---

[62] To do a bunk is to leave rapidly or escape, generally to avoid some unwanted development.

[63] Colman's had been producing mustard in Norwich since 1814. The policy of firing women when they got married was standard practice in many companies at this time. Otherwise, Colman's had a reputation of providing excellent social benefits, including company housing, to its employees. Incidentally, the logbook of Ethel's school records how a teacher's employment was terminated on her marriage.

know that job either, but she stood next to me and I learned her it. After that she earned money, but she was a long time without a job, 'cause I was only little when she got married.

Once you started work you had to pay insurance money.[64] That was cut out of your wages every week. It was a stamp what you got. If you got a complaint and you couldn't go to work, you went *on the club*. You'd have to go and sign down at the Norwich Union and you'd get a little out of the sick money. But that was only if you were sick for more than four days. If you belonged to the boot and shoe operatives, you'd get a little extra out of that. But six or seven shillings at the most. One time, my brother Billy was on the club. He'd been ill for about a week. I think he'd had bad tonsillitis. Well, he was in love with his young lady, Edie, and one evening he said he felt better and he was going to see her. She lived up Golden Ball Street, near the newspapers. Mother said: 'Now hurry up and don't get home late.' But just as he went this bloke, the 'sick man',[65] come to the door. They would have stopped his money straight away if he weren't home. So, Mother told him that Billy was in the toilet, and asked him into the living room for

[64] Most workers paid a few pence per week into an unemployment insurance scheme. Once unemployed though the benefits were paid for only a relatively short period of time – ten weeks in the case of the Norwich boot and shoe operatives. Once these benefits were exhausted, those without work had to throw themselves on the mercy of the local authorities. The homeless and absolutely destitute could be taken into the workhouse where they would be given Spartan and segregated accommodation and a meagre food allowance. Others could receive a small weekly allowance if they satisfied a harsh and hated means test. Since these payments to the unemployed were paid for out of local taxation (the rates), the authorities were always under great popular pressure to keep them as low as possible.

[65] Inspectors would make unannounced visits to the homes of those drawing unemployment benefits to verify that were genuinely incapable of work and not abusing the system.

a cup of tea. Then she got Charlie, my brother what's two years older than me, in the front room and said: 'Go and get Billy.' And all the while, Mother kept talking to the man. When Billy got back, he went straight into the toilet. He took his braces off and stripped himself, 'cause when they went with a girl they always put on a nice tie and shirt. And then he came in from the back in his work clothes. That man must have thought there were something wrong with him in the toilet all that time, but he couldn't prove nothing, could he?

When we were kids, we didn't know nothing about politics. We didn't know the Labour candidate, but because we were poor, we thought we ought to vote for him. Mr Cutmore was the Conservative candidate – Mr Cutmore the baker. He had the baker's office in Barrack Street, and I suppose they had a nice house as well. Very distinguished people, really, but they were rich and we were poor. So we used to go round singing:

> Vote, vote, vote for Mr (the Labour candidate).
> Chuck old Cutmore in the bin,
> Cause he in't no bloomin' good,
> And he's like a block of wood,
> So we don't vote for him any more.

⋅⊰⊱⋅

When I was a little girl, I used to dream that I had a wealthy father and mother. I used to think, 'I'm not really in this family'. And one day they're going to come and get me and take me to this big beautiful house. Of course, I didn't really want anyone to come and get me, but I did like going to Uncle Billy's house.

My Uncle Billy and Aunt Sally were our posh relations. They lived in a lovely house in Helena Road between the Dereham and Earlham

Roads. It had an entrance hall and carpets. The furniture was all antique stuff, but that was good. In the front room there was a bowl that went round and round when you touched it. And there were all lovely vases and carpet on the stairs. Uncle Billy was very big and he had a gruff voice. He weren't what you'd call a smart man. He was coarse-looking and he had a rough, wrinkly face, though he weren't an old gentleman. His appearance was the same as what his inside was. He was sort of gruesome, if you know what I mean. Aunt Sally was a nice-looking lady, a little busky[66] woman with a lovely face and her hair all up. She always told Mother: 'If anything happen to him before me, I'll see you right, Nelly.' But, of course, my mother died before him. Sad really.

Every summer, Aunt Sally used to say: 'Nelly, I'll have Ethel round for a week.' And I used to think: 'I'm going to have a whole egg of my own. And all that lovely food.' Aunt Sally made Yorkshire pudding. I never even knew how to make them when I got married, 'cause we never had 'em at home. The oven weren't big enough. And Aunt Sally had fruit what we didn't have at home. Bananas and apples. That was a treat. Oh it was lovely. You were out of one world into another. It was like a fairyland to me. I was a little princess there. Aunt Sally bathed me and looked after me. Their children were married so I had all the attention. And it were so quiet, 'cause there were only him and her. And I can't remember him being about that much.

The bedroom she put me in was done out beautifully – a little wooden bed with a lovely counterpane on it, and a pretty pillow. But

[66] buxom

the first few nights I went there, I couldn't sleep. I used to look outside the window and see the cemetery and the graves. And I kept thinking that these 'ere ghosts were going to come out. And the thing of it is I don't know why she put me in that back bedroom because she had a middle bedroom with no one sleeping in it. I didn't want her to know how frightened I was, but when it was time to go to bed one night, I said: 'Oh Aunt Sally, I'm frightened. I look over the cemetery.' Of course they didn't have electricity, but after that she give me this candle. You had it in a saucer and that would last the whole night. Of course all the things were still out there, but I didn't worry 'cause this light was on. We never had no candles at home, but there was a lot of us, weren't there? So I was never alone.

Aunt Sally had a dressing gown. It was pale blue with a sash. We never knew such things in our house. And she had slippers. At home, we just took our boots and shoes off and put them under the couch. We never had no slippers. I'd go skipping outside in the dressing gown and slippers. The children round there were so posh, but I didn't care about that. We'd play hopscotch, and then Aunt Sally would say: 'Come on Ethel.' And I'd sit up at this posh table all on my own and have this lovely breakfast. There was always a whole egg for me, and lovely bread and butter cut into soldiers. Another thing I liked was playing shop in their shed. They had chickens, a big bag of maize, and scales there. I'd say: 'Good morning, Mrs Brown. You want your usual order? Oh I don't think I can let you have anything because you haven't paid for last week's.' Aunt Sally used to be listening to me. She'd be roaring with laughter, and she'd say: 'Oh, you'll be the death of me.'

In them days, there was a lot of respectable people. We lived in very hard conditions, but the majority were people what kept themselves clean. None of us had anything much. We couldn't say: 'Oh, her over there, she got more than me.' We were all in the same boat. But us what lived in the terraced houses had it a lot better than them poor unfortunates what lived up the yards.[67] In my day, there was loads of these yards all over Norwich. We had a six-roomed house. We had three bedrooms. We had our own copper to wash our linen. We had an oven in the wall, and we had our own toilet. But these people up the yards, they had nothing. They lived in two-roomed or one-roomed houses and there was no sanitary. No water inside. I never even saw a window in the one-roomed houses. You opened the door and went down the steps, and the smell was horrific. But they didn't have nothing to keep them clean. The mother and father and all the children slept in the same room. And some had to sleep mothers and fathers and kids in one bed.

[67] The yards were areas of sub-standard dilapidated housing, built around a small central courtyard in which could be found the communal tap or water pump and pit lavatories. The yards were approached through narrow passageways from the road – the approach from Barrack Street to Black Boys Yard, a few hundred yards from Ethel's, was only about four feet wide. There are several contemporary accounts that describe the yards as being strewn with filth and rubbish and with drains blocked and overflowing. Most of them were cobbled which made cleaning difficult. Many of the yards in Norwich dated back two hundred years or more from Ethel's time, but those in her immediate area had been put up in the second half of the nineteenth century to house the country people that were flowing into the city as unemployment in the rural areas was rising. The builders could have run water to each home, but that would have been an expense too much.

The Floods of 1912

Magdalen Street

Heigham Street

In 1912 the yards were all flooded out. I weren't born, but I've heard my mother and my sisters talking about it.[68] Terrific storms, water gushing down from the top of the hill, running down the street like a river. And it couldn't get away. There were drains, but they weren't always kept clear, and the water just ran over them. We were all right, 'cause we were on the slope. But them poor things in the yards at the bottom there, they got all flooded out.

The people in the yards tried to do their best, but they didn't really have a chance. They sometimes didn't know where the next penny was coming from, especially if the man was sick. He usually had to go back to work before he was well, 'cause otherwise his job would be taken. They were undernourished and most of them weren't healthy.[69] A lot had horrible sores, big yellow sores on their faces and on their lips, little children with eyes, red and yellow.

The women in the yards wore aprons made out of old sackcloth. And you could see that their blouses had been worn for weeks and weeks. They wore old caps on their head, like a man's cap, and their hairs were anyhow. A lot of the children never had nothing on their

---

[68] From 26-27 August 1912, torrential rain fell continuously for 29 hours depositing 7¾ inches of water, 6 inches of which fell in less than 12 hours. The City drainage system could not cope and massive flooding resulted. Water levels rose almost three times higher than the worst previous flood, the Candlemas flood of 1570. The memories of Ethel's family about the impact of the flood in the nearby 'yards' are correct. The *Daily Citizen* later wrote: '[Norwich] has literally hundreds of little, narrow, sunless courts, resembling nothing more than a series of rabbit runs, and the dampness which the waters left as legacy has never disappeared'.

[69] The poor health of many of Ethel's schoolmates emerges clearly from the following entries from the St Saviour's School logbook: October 1922 – 'During this 4 days a total of 144 girls were examined of whom 66 were recommended for definite treatment or observation with regard to physique, dental trouble or cleanliness.' September 1923 – 'School dentist examined ... girls...91 recommended for treatment.' March 4, 1926 – 'The head teacher discovered this morning that over 40 children, out of 170 present, had come to school with no proper breakfast and without sitting down to the table.'

feet. They used to give them shoes at school from time to time, but a lot of the mothers and fathers would pawn 'em or sell 'em. It was a sad thing. The boys had short trousers with all the behind out of them, and their shirts didn't look as if they'd been washed for ages. There were some women that tried. You used to see them Saturday afternoon with their curling pins all over their head. They didn't even cover them up. They'd probably go out the night time. Though they were poor, they always used to find the money to have a drink on a Saturday or Sunday night.

They had to share the facilities in the yards. A few toilets, a washhouse, and one copper for twenty houses. You couldn't just go in and turn the tap on. You had to get pails of water. And there weren't no turning the gas on. You had to get stuff to light the copper. And then, when you'd done, you couldn't just run the dirty water out. You had to scoop it out. Well, there were some of them women what left the dirty water in. And that's when a lot of the trouble started. You see, with the houses all round the yard, the doors were all facing each other. And because there weren't nothing to be in for, the people would nearly always be sitting outside. So that meant that everyone could see who went in the washhouse last. One woman would accuse another. Then they'd start shouting and abusing each other, until all of a sudden they'd explode. One would fly for the other and they'd be fighting. They pulled each other's hair and hit one another with their hands. We'd all go to watch. As soon as someone say: 'There's a fight going on up the yards,' all us kids from Cavalry Street and Mousehold Street run down to have a look. It didn't frighten us, 'cause it weren't gruesome in any way. They weren't ferocious women. They just had a lot on their plate. They didn't have enough money to manage on.

They lived in appalling conditions, and little things got them down. That was all trivial, but they didn't have anything to take their mind off it.[70] They talk about stress today, but they don't know what stress is. I realise now what a job it was, but when I was young I didn't think nothing about it. I just thought, oh those people up them yards.

There weren't no ovens in the houses in the yards, so on Sunday mornings you'd see the women all coming out with their square tins and their bits of meat, going to get them cooked in the baker's oven in Barrack Street. All for tuppence. I don't think they had much to eat the majority of the week, but most of them had a good Sunday dinner. You know like you make a joint and you put your onion in. And we used to have gravy salt in them days. Sprinkle it on and stir it. The baker's oven held more than thirty dinners. There was an art in cooking all of them. The old baker had to keep going in to look. If a dinner was doing too much, he'd bring that one forward. He had something that looked like a flat wood spade with a long, long handle. If the gravy was getting short on one, he used to get his big spoon and nick a bit out of another. So someone who had pork might end up with some rabbit gravy. They used to go after their dinners about one o'clock.

There was a woman what lived in one of the yards. She was like a long doll with a black skirt. And she wore a hat, like a sort of witch's

[70] Several cases of fights between women of the type that Ethel witnessed ended up in Court. The *Norwich Mercury* of December 29, 1920, reported that 'At Norwich Police Court last Friday, Jessie Crooks of 6 Sportsman's Yard, Barrack Street was summoned by Nellie Cooper, who alleged assault…Defendant admitted striking complainant, but alleged the latter sent her a dirty, insulting letter. On oath, Cooper denied sending the letter. The Magistrate's Clerk – "You have made a mistake". Defendant was fined 5/-.' Earlier that year, a woman from Houghton's Yard was also fined 5/- for having taken a woman 'by the throat and knelt on her'. She told the Court that she would never be able to find such a sum and so would have to go to prison instead.

Norwich Yards

Severns Yard

Gaffer's Yard

Black Boys Yard

Holmes's Yard

hat. I heard she come from a rich family, and her people had put her out because she had something wrong with her nose. Well, she didn't really have a nose. Just a pinky cardboard one. She used to go round with her husband. They sold bootlaces, matches and the *Beano*.[71] He called out for people to buy with his gruff voice, but you never saw her speak or nothing. Poor woman. I don't know what happened to her. The kids used to call her 'old no-nose'. They didn't go behind her and shout. No, I never seen anyone abuse her like that. But they'd say: 'Have you seen old no-nose today?' Which wasn't a very nice thing, but when you're kids, you say things like that.

Mrs Noakes lived in that yard. She must have been a nice woman in her time, but when I knew her she wasn't very good looking because she'd had a family and got old. Her hair was all straggly, but in that day no one had their hair done. You just cut it yourself and you washed it with carbolic soap. It was the cheapest soap you could get, and it smelt horrible. Mrs Noakes didn't have a husband at home, but she weren't a widow. I saw her husband once. Whether he hit her I don't know, but they were having a squabble and he caused a lot of trouble. In the end, Mrs Noakes shoved him out and locked the door. He was blind drunk, hanging around the two posts outside our house. He was there for a good while and then he went off.[72] So, she never

---

[71] A popular weekly comic for children.

[72] Ethel's memories of Mr Noakes are borne out by contemporary sources. On December 18, 1920, under the headline 'Good Luck to You – Cheerful Toper and the Policeman', The *Norwich Mercury* reported: 'At Norwich Police Court on Thursday Henry Noakes (42) labourer of 15 Green Yard, Barrack Street was charged with being drunk and disorderly in Barrack Street, Wednesday. PC Wanbon said he saw accused on Wednesday night and cautioned him. He was drunk and shouted obscene language. Witness arrested him and when formally charged, he said "Good luck to you!" The Chairman (Mr C.F.Hinde) said this was the third time Noakes had been up in six weeks.... In this case he was fined £1. Time for payment was allowed.'

really was a widow. And she couldn't have had a pension, because they didn't give you no pension till your husband died, did they? And she got nothing for the children. The family allowance hadn't come out in that time.

The poor lady struggled. She had four children, and they were brought up poor. They were pale, and they went to school with fleabites on their necks. Mrs Noakes used to go around selling matches and bootlaces. She was absolutely down and out, but at least she kept a roof over their heads. Then one day there was no door. 'Mrs Noakes got her door off,' I say to Mother. 'They say she couldn't pay the rent.' I expect the rent man, whoever he was, thought: 'If I take her door off, she'll find something.' Well, they all had to go to bed and leave it like that, and it weren't the summer time. Of course, you didn't hear so much about robbing in them days, 'cause there was nothing to rob.

Some of the worst-treated women were them what come from the workhouse. Most of the girls in there would go with anyone. They didn't care who they married so long as they got out, 'cause it was scrubbing from morning to night. A lady who I used to know told me that's where her husband got her from. They used to do that, years ago. If they wanted a wife and they couldn't get one, they'd go to the workhouse. This lady's husband was very rough and ready. Not a very nice man for such an elegant lady. No way would she have had him, you'd have thought, but I expect she was just glad to get out. Of course, it all had to be done legally. They couldn't just get them out of the workhouse and leave them to their own resources. A man could only get a wife if he could take care of her.

8. Drinking

In them days, most people liked a drink. Now where the men got the money I don't know. They were poor and they didn't have good jobs. Beer was tuppence a pint, which was a lot of money really, 'cause you could get a pint of milk or a loaf of bread for the same price. But they were like my father. They always found money for drinks and smokes. That's why a lot of them didn't bring enough money home, and why the women didn't have as much as they should have had. Of course, there were some nice men, who didn't come home drunk, but in most households the father was drunk. You wouldn't see it quite so much in the week, but Saturdays you'd see all these little men – they always seemed to be little men – you'd see them coming up the road and they'd be wobbling one side to the other. You weren't frightened or anything. I think they didn't really mean to get drunk, but it happened. They lived in terrible conditions, and that brought the worst out of them. Most of them went to have a drink to get away from the poverty. I'm sure that's why my father went out. The thing of it was, there was nothing else for 'em. The majority of them didn't want to go to the pictures and with a house full of children, what could they do at home? Some of the wives used to go Saturday evenings with their husbands and have a bottle of stout or pale ale. But there wasn't many women what got drunk. They didn't have the money. It was the men what were earning, and they were at the pub every night.

Fighting in the street was a way of life, especially weekends. They'd all be in the pub and when it was turning out time, they'd got so much drink in them, they'd start the fights. They'd come right into the street near the pawnshop. We could see them from our window. They stripped to the waist and fought bare-fisted. The next day they'd all be together again. Perhaps a couple had black eyes, and another had a cut on his mouth or something, but they'd be good old friends. There was one family in particular. They used to go out together to the pub, all happy, but as soon as they got drink down 'em they'd start to quarrel. And they always ended up the night fighting, the women and all. The next morning there'd be black eyes and what have you, but they'd all be pals again.

One day I was coming down Anchor Street, and I saw this big man what lived up the yards. He was shaking Pimper Wiley round the neck, Pimper Wiley what lived a few doors down from us. I don't know why we called him that. Perhaps he had a red nose. All I can remember is that he was a character. The house he took was a shop previous. And he had a lot of antiques. He was a nice man, and he used to let us kids go in. We went down two steps to his living room. He had this big basin what they used to bath babies in years ago – a hand basin and jug. He used to take the jug out, and somehow that used to go round and round, and that fascinated us. I don't think he spoke to us much. He was just a friendly, nice man, very tall and thin. He had no relatives that I know of. No wife, no children. I can remember walking past his place this day and, through the window, I saw a man, a big man, shaking him, a big bully of a man. He might have had too much to drink, or he might have went round to tell Pimper off for something. And then maybe Pimper said something out of turn, and he lost his temper. I don't know, but that was a horrifying thing for a little girl to see. Then, the next minute, poor Pimper's head was through the glass window. Why he never got his throat cut, I don't know. I can remember him pulling his neck out, and there weren't a bit of blood. I don't know exactly how it happened. Whether the man intended Pimper to go through the window I don't know. Maybe he was angry and got his throat and pushed him, thinking that was a wall and not a window. But if he'd pushed him in the wall, he'd have bashed his head in wouldn't he?

When some men got drink in them, they went home and upset the women and children. There was a lot of that went on. You'd go past houses and hear kids screaming, 'cause the father and mother were fighting. One day in Barrack Street, I saw a woman screaming and her husband chasing her. Probably she'd done nothing wrong. In that day a woman didn't have to do nothing wrong for her husband to knock her about. Like I told you, when Father first married Mother, he used to come in and hit her for nothing. Till she woke up one day and she hit him back. But there was not everyone could do that. There wasn't many women could stand up to the men, especially them with children. They didn't have enough food to be boisterous. When you went out, you'd see a lot of them with black eyes. The women were the weak link, and the men were the governors.

My friend, Violet Littleboy, used to tell me about a family what lived up a yard in Cowgate Street. Every Saturday, the man used to come home drunk about ten or eleven o'clock at night. O' course the pubs weren't open after ten, so they had to come in then. And he'd go in the house, knock his wife about, and then shove them all out in the street. I know that for a fact, cause Violet told me. 'He come home drunk again last night,' she'd say. 'Turned all the poor kids out in the street, and the mother, in their nightdresses.' In summer, in winter, with snow on the ground. And that was just one family. There were thousands like that, all over the country.

There was a couple what lived in a caravan in a big yard next to the old second hand shop. He must have been older than her. I don't know whether she was a Gypsy, but that's the type of person you would term her as. She used to go out and sell magazines, and shoelaces and matches. And they had this little boy. He had a donkey and he used to run it up and down the street. They did that in them days. He used to say bad words and I was terrified of him. They were quiet enough normally, but one Saturday, someone said to me: 'Mrs So-and-So's going through the streets shouting. She's been drinking all day.' By the time she got home, the husband had heard all about it and started whipping her. We were in bed, but when I heard the commotion, I went through to the boys' room. I asked Billy: 'Whatever is it?' She weren't screaming, she was moaning. We could hear the whip. Oh, I couldn't bear it, but my brother said: 'There's nothing you can do about it.' I put my hands over my ears.

There was a lady what lived in one of the little houses near the Church in Barrack Street. She was in her late fifties. One day when I was going past her house, she was shouting, and the man was shouting. Now you know, when you're kids, you're all ears. And this wasn't a house up a yard. The door was on the pavement where you walked, so I could see right in. Then, all of a sudden, she come out with these ornaments off the mantelpiece and started throwing them onto the ground. Then she went in and got some more. She must have cleared her mantelpiece. She was telling her husband how she felt about his drinking, but I don't suppose she ever got them ornaments replaced. They didn't have money did they?

My father was a very clever little man, a lovely man, but he would drink. It was a sad thing. Whatever made him do it? He was a steady, good, wonderful bricklayer and he used to have big men all over Norwich come and get him to do all sorts of brick work and tiling. Even some of the churches used to have him. You see, he had it up there, and he could earn a lot of money. He could have built houses. He could have been his own governor. But as soon as he earned the money, he'd spend it on his drink. He worked for Bush, the builder, but he should really have been his partner. Bush used to be Father's apprentice when he was a young boy. Father was the one what shew him what to do. But Bush saved his money and bought a little business. Mother used to say: 'That could have been Bush and Edwards.' And that would have been good, 'cause then father could have had his sons work for him. He could have had all them boys bricklayers. He could have learned them all. One day, Mother said to him: 'My boys aren't all going to be labourers. At least one of 'em is going to be a professional, 'cause labourers' money is nothing.' And that was how Charlie come to be a bricklayer.[73]

Every couple of years or so, Father was called out to repair the baker's oven. He used to go round on a Sunday morning early, and he took my two brothers for labourers. He'd have to get right in the oven. It must have been claustrophobic, 'cause them ovens only had little

---

[73] To become a skilled craftsman, it was essential to serve an apprenticeship. The apprentice would agree to go for several years on little or no income while he learned his trade by working directly with his skilled master. In many cases, in addition to the low income, an apprentice would have to make an upfront payment to the master for taking him on. Many poor families could not afford to pay this and many were unwilling to pass up the chance of an additional labourer's wage being added immediately to the household budget.

Mother and Father

doors. He told me: 'It's like being in an oxo[74] when you get in there.' And them ovens never got cold. When they come home they was black, like they'd been dipped in a bag of soot. They used to get about five pound for the job, but it never benefited us. Father'd give my brothers something each for helping him, and then he'd take the week off and get drunk.

Father didn't always come home drunk, but he was at the pub every night of the week. The worst days were when he didn't go to work. Bricklayers today can work in bad weather, 'cause they put something in the cement. But in them days when it rained or snowed, Father couldn't work. When the kids were little, he used to go out and chop wood for bread when that happened. But when most of 'em were earning I suppose he thought: 'I don't need to go chopping wood, 'cause they're all at home giving her board.' So, for most of the winter, he wasn't working. And on the days when he didn't go to work, he was drinking. He'd go out early in the morning and stay out all day in the pub. With a crowd of children in the house, he didn't want to be at home. Mother would have his dinner on all day, and it'd be boiling and boiling. I don't know why she never learned, because he never come home until late.

As soon as it was getting near ten, my heart would start beating. 'Please Heavenly Father, don't let him come home drunk.' But of course he did. I'd look at the clock, and I'd say: 'Mother, shall we go to bed.' But when she got in that mood, poor lady, she couldn't have gone to sleep anyway. She used to get a bit jealous, thinking he'd been with other women, 'cause you can't be in a pub all the time. And that

[74] A brown crumbly bouillon cube.

upset her greatly. When he did come home, she used to say: 'You've been in someone's house. You haven't been in a pub all day.' She used to say some horrible things, but he was one of them men, what was happy-go-lucky when he was drunk. 'I've had a day with my pals today,' he'd sing, and that used to rile her even more. 'You old b.,' she used to say. 'You ought to have been with me. I'm your pal. I don't know why you want to be out all day. I've had your dinner on since morning. Why in't you been in?' And he used to laugh and say: 'Ask the dog, ask the dog.'

It was horrible for a little girl to see. He'd been in different pubs all day long and he'd be rolling about all over the place. As soon as he got in, I'd say: 'Father, let me take your boots off.' I wanted to get him upstairs out of Mother's way so they didn't quarrel. He'd go up three stairs and fall down four. She'd say: 'You want to break your neck,' and she really meant it. She'd go up after him. And they'd be arguing and arguing, and I couldn't sleep. All I was doing was clasping my little hands and praying: 'Please God, don't let them fight.' I was frightened of the dark, but when it all went quiet, I had to get out of bed and go to their room. Father was snoring because he was drunk. But Mother? Was she breathing? I'd go right near her face. And she'd say: 'What are you doing, Ethel?' 'Oh I just wanted a drink of water, Mother,' I'd say. She always had a jug of water by the bed at night time, in case any of us kids wanted a drink. It's so pathetic, a little girl getting out of bed at night, 'cause she wanted to see if her Mother was alive. They never did fight in front of me, but I was always frightened that they were going to. I felt secure the nights my brother Billy wasn't out courting. I knew Mother wouldn't say too much to Father when Billy was there.

Father had hundreds of pubs he went to, and he never let no-one know where he was. Mother used to say to him: 'If anything happen to any of 'em, I won't know where to find you.' And that used to worry her. If one of us had got killed, she'd have to wait till he come home drunk that night to tell him. My sister told me that one time Mother went after him. I don't think it were for money. She wouldn't lower herself that way. But this particular time, he'd been out all day and she'd got herself into a stew. She went all round Norwich in the pubs. She had one baby in her arms and she was carrying another, you know, in her stomach. In the end, she found him in a pub at the bottom of Kett's Hill. He wouldn't come straight away and as she got going home, she tripped and broke her ankle. So, she had to drag herself all the way home with a broken ankle, and a baby on her arm.

Father used to do a lot of work for businesses. And sometimes, some of these builders what he knew were in the pub with him. They weren't gentry. They were just ordinary men what had made a lot of money through building. Sometimes when Father was really drunk, they'd bring him home. They'd come to the door and Mother would offer them tuppence. They say: 'Oh no, it's all right. We know old Mike.' (I don't know why they used to call him Mike.) 'He done a lot of good work for us. We don't like seeing him drunk in the road.' Barrack Street was notorious at certain times. They were a rough lot of men down there. Them they didn't know, they knocked 'em about for a couple of bob, or fivepence or thruppence. They'd even set about the soldiers. Sometimes, Mother would put on her cape and go to look for Father. She weren't afraid. She say: 'I'm looking for my husband, Albert Edwards.' 'Ooh,' they say: 'we know him. We won't touch him.'

One week when Father had been a nuisance, the older boys got to hear of it. I don't know how. That Saturday, my brothers and sisters came round to ours. They used to come most Saturdays. That would be past ten when the pubs shut. They'd bring their own fish and chips, and Mother would cut the bread, and butter it up, and give them the salt and vinegar. And she'd get them cups of tea. She didn't need all that. Poor old dear. This particular night, I was abed and I could hear them shouting at Father and telling him off. They were furious with him for treating Mother like that. Sam was really getting on to Father. It might have come to blows, but then I came running downstairs. 'Leave him alone. Don't you touch my father.' And ooh, Sam give me a big swipe across the face. No-one said: 'Why did you do it?' But then mother stepped in. She told 'em all: 'Look, I can dictate to your father, but I don't want none of you coming and telling him what to do. If you want to come here and have a social time and a cup of cocoa, you can. But if you come, you respect me, and you don't interfere with your Father. I can take him to do, but not you lot.' They all went quiet, but they never got onto Father no more.

It's a sad thing that Fred and Albert were drinkers like Father. You see when they were young, he was too drunk to be worrying about what they were doing. Albert would come in drunk and Mother couldn't do nothing about it. Then one day, he had a terrible accident at work and he got compensation. But instead of him putting some money away for a rainy day, the silly boy used to go and drink it away like Father. He used to go to the pub every night and get drunk. He'd fall down, and all his money, half crowns and two-shilling pieces, would roll in the street. My sisters told me how they used to go and pick them up.

One time Fred and Albert met up and went out drinking. They came back to ours about nine thirty and they'd both had a lot to drink. Nelly and Charlie and Frank and me were there. We were playing ever so nice, but then Fred and Albert come in and started pinching Frank 'cause he was so fat. Of course he was fat, but they didn't have to do that. Frank was a big boy, but he go boo-hoo. That broke my heart, and I ran to the pub to get Mother and Father. I was like a little greyhound. Mother was having a stout and Father was having a couple of pints. 'Come home,' I said. 'They're upsetting our Frankie.' Well of course they come down and Father told 'em off. Now if Albert would have just went to bed and Fred had gone home where he belonged, then Father would have been all right. If only they didn't argue, it would have been all right. But they did, and Father said: 'That's it. Both of you get out. You an' all Albert.' So Albert had to go home with Fred 'cause he didn't have nowhere else to go. After I got older I did feel sad that I ran after Father and Mother that night, but I had to do it because poor Frank, he was crying. I was always a bit afraid of Albert. He was a bit aggressive and I think he never liked me after that night. I hope he forgive me when he see me in Heaven.

Poor Albert. I think his life was sort of doomed. He had a good home and a good mother, but he was a poor little boy in a way. Although he was our brother, he must have had that inferior thing about Mother and Father. Especially when people called him Chaplin, and all the rest of us were Edwards. I should imagine people perhaps said things to him. Poor boy. He must have been sad at times, which I didn't realize when I was young. You know, he wet the bed right until he was a man. And he had to sleep with my brothers, didn't he? Mother put something on the bed to try and protect the others, but you can bet they suffered a bit, didn't they? But that wasn't his fault. Years ago, people used to punish their children for that. But Mother, she never mentioned it. In all my life I never, never heard her tell him off for anything. I think she felt sorry for him. But when he used to come home a lot the worse for drink, that didn't help his complaint.

Some years later Frank come home drunk one night. He must have been about sixteen or seventeen. He'd went with some boys and he come home sicking everywhere. Father was almost never home, but he was in bed this particular night, and he was furious. He got up and when he saw Frank like this, he must have thought: 'I don't want a repeat of Fred and Albert. I'll stop this 'ere now.' So he hit him. He hit him with his hand, not a belt. I don't think my father ever wore a belt. I was horrified, but there was nothing I could do about it. I put my fingers in my ears. That was the only time I ever known my Father to hit any of them. He'd shout at you if you were naughty but I never saw him raise a hand to any of them. I don't remember Frank ever coming home like that again.

When Walter was seven, I heard he came home one day and said: 'I've joined the Salvation Army.' I don't know why he did. It might have been all that drunkenness.[75] Mother got all the brothers together and said: 'Now look, Walter has joined the Salvation Army and I don't

[75] During Victorian times and the early part of the twentieth century, drink provided workers with some escape from the harshness of their lives, but often at a terrible cost. Not only were drinkers prone to be violent to their families, they frequently spent so much of their pitifully small wages in public houses that their families went hungry or were evicted from their homes. To combat this evil, from the early nineteenth century, a nationwide temperance movement developed that brought together activists from churches, unions and various other social reform groups. Among the Christian groups, the Salvation Army was probably the most ardent. Founded in 1865, the Army organized itself along military lines in its battle against the demon drink. All members were required to be absolute teetotallers. It is understandable how uncomfortable Walter became at family gatherings where the drinks flowed freely (see p 126).

want any of you to laugh at him. I want you to respect him. If you don't, you'll get the hiding of your lives, 'cause I'm not having that boy ridiculed.' We were a rough and ready family, but we did respect Walter. When he was home, we were all religious. We didn't put a step wrong. I remember walking out one Saturday afternoon. I was only a little girl, and there was my brother Walter, and crowds round him. He was standing on a big thing, giving a sermon. He had his lovely uniform on, and he really looked the part. And I can remember these words that kept with me. 'Jesus didn't come on the earth wrapped in cotton wool. He came on the earth, as a man, and He came to do all these lovely, wonderful things.' I can't remember no more about it, but that stuck in my mind. And listened, and I thought: 'Oh that's my brother.' His voice was lovely, soft and educated. I would have liked to have heard him preach a lot more, but we didn't go to hear him.

After Walter got married to Eva, he got into Davey Place post office. He done well, 'cause it was a job to get in. When he first started working there, they didn't know whether they liked him or not. I suppose they thought, oh we've got a religious crank here. I say to him one time: 'How you getting on, Walter?' And he said: 'I'm all right sister. I'm fine. They call me Halleluiah.' 'Why do they do that?' I say. 'Well, when I first went there, they used to laugh at me and make fun of me. And I just used to turn round and say, "Halleluia". And after that, they all called me Halleluiah.' But he didn't get upset. He always kept his cool, always kept religious as he should. And that's why they respected him, why they liked him. Walter never seemed to have any money. But when he died, his son, Herbert, said that all the while, he was giving it away. Charities, charities, charities. That's what he did. I'm sure he's well up there. I hope he'll come and meet me when I go.

Walter's wedding

9. Shopping

There was a little shop on each corner. Mrs Howlett's was opposite us. And it was immaculate. In winter, you'd look out of the window at night, and you'd see it lit up in the snow. There was a little bell on the door, and you could hear it from early morning 'till ten o'clock at night. Poor people, they didn't have a lot of rest. The window was always very tempting, with the sweets and chocolates placed very neat and clean. When we didn't have no money we just stood looking. Sometimes, I'd say: 'Mother, give us a penny.' And if she had one, she'd sometimes say: 'Oh all right.' And I'd go running across the road. 'Please can I have a penn'orth of toffee with nuts in?' Well blow me, I got my weight in toffee, but Mrs Howlett used to be taking the nuts out and eating them. I can see her now, champing on them. She was a plump lady, and her husband was tall and dark with a little moustache. They both wore glasses. They didn't have no family, but they were lovely people. Their customers didn't just go in to buy, they liked a bit of gossip an' all. That weren't malicious or anything, but they all liked to know what was going on.

For a penny you could buy a flycatcher, a candle or two oranges. Sugar, marge, carrots, parsnips, turnips, apples and pears were all tuppence a pound. A quarter of sweets, a quarter of a stone of potatoes, a cabbage, a cauliflower, a glass of pickled onions, a packet of crisps, a stalk of Brussels sprouts (they were always sold on the stalk then) or a bag of soda for wash day, they all cost tuppence. Flour was fourpence a bag and so was a pound of tomatoes or a quarter of best sweets. Grapes cost sixpence a pound. We never could afford them.

Sally and Thursy Winter were sisters. They had a corner shop too, and they sold nearly everything. 'Run up the road,' my brothers used to say to me, 'and get us a packet of Woodbines'.[76] Howlett's was right near, but I wouldn't go there. I'd run up to Sally and Thursy's. It were extra time, but I didn't care. Mr and Mrs Howlett didn't give nothing away, but Sally and Thursy would always give you sweets. They were both lovely ladies. Thursy was big, with rosy cheeks and reddish hair and Sally was a little dark woman with sharp features. When Nelly and I used to play shops, she was Sally and I was Thursy. I used to say: 'Well, what do you think, Sally? Should we let this lady have some more goods?' And Nelly'd say: 'Well, I don't know. She in't paid her bill.' So I'd say: 'Well, we'll do it just this one time.'

Mrs Cossey was on the corner over the road. She had a baker's, and a provisional shop. My brother, Fred, worked there for a while. He used to make the dough for the bread. Later, he died of cancer, and I think it must have been the flour. The fourth corner was the Robin Hood and a bit further on, there was a shop what the people lived in. The man used to do men's shoes, but after a while they got out, and there was a fish shop there. But that weren't never very successful 'cause everyone liked the one at the bottom of Anchor Street. Mr Harvey, what owned it, was a big man. His wife was a sprightly little woman, and as clean as a new pin. She would serve right quick, but she always had big queues, especially Friday nights when people got paid. On the corner opposite Mrs Harvey's, there was a second hand shop. Parks I think the name was, and they had this

---

[76] *Woodbines* were the cheapest brand of cigarettes generally available. They first appeared in 1888, the first cigarettes to be produced by a new automated process that greatly undercut the prices of those produced by the traditional methods.

girl. Posie her name was. She was about eighteen. I don't know why, but she befriended me and I used to love her. They had a lovely old piano in the shop, and she used to let me go in and play it. That smelt horrible, 'cause there was all old second hand clothes, blankets, fur coats, boots and shoes. That weren't like the Oxfam shops today, with all that nearly-new stuff. Them old things in Parks' used to smell terrible. Pooh, I can smell it now. But I didn't care then. I just wanted to play on that piano.

Mother sometimes used to give us a ha'penny and we'd go to this lovely sweet shop called Pearson's.[77] Mrs Pearson was a dark woman, and big. I don't remember a man ever being there. You could have two ounces of sweets for a penny. But in the window, she had what we called Dirty Mixtures. Mother never knew nothing about them, and of course, we didn't tell her. They were fly-blown sweets, the ones what had been in the window what Mrs Pearson couldn't sell. You could get a big bag of 'em for a ha'penny. There were all sorts in it. Sugared almonds, (they were expensive so we only ever got the fly-blown ones), jellies, a bit of chocolate. Once I got a pin in mine. Where that come from, I don't know. Maybe she'd stuck the price on the sweets with it. That was an ordinary pin, but if you got it stuck in your throat, it

---

[77] In Ethel's childhood, sweets were sold from big jars. Among the most popular boiled sweets were gobstoppers (a real choking hazard – almost as big as a golf ball) that changed colours as you sucked them, aniseed balls (that had to be sucked to the end to get to the seed), pear drops (that tasted like the smell of nail-varnish remover), and rosebuds (small pink and white sweets that tasted of rosewater). Then there were various types of toffee – notably stickjaw and chewies. Other popular varieties included buttered brazils, snowballs, brandy balls, Fry's five boys chocolate bars, licorice shoelaces, and white sugar mice with string tails. Then there were exotic sounding varieties such as Jap nuggets. On winter days, sweets made from horehound or eucalyptus were popular. Children could also buy very cheaply lengths of the fibrous licorice plant that they would chew to extract the flavour. Dried locust bean pods were just as cheap and chewed in similar fashion.

wouldn't be very nice would it? Of course, we knew they weren't clean. But I'm alive to tell the tale.

Billy's wife's mother used to keep a little shop in her front room. They used to do that in them days. They'd have a window with them glass jars. A few mixtures here and a few chocolates there. I used to like going round to hers, 'cause she used to give me sweets. A couple of doors up from ours, there was another sweetshop in a house. The little old lady had a counter and all the sweets in the front room window. She used to have to stand on a box because she was a hunchback, bless her. We used to call her 'little hunchy'.

Beatty Royal's mother had a shop. It was a nice little shop. She wouldn't have Dirty Mixtures or anything like that. I never remember getting anything myself, but I was in there once when one of the kids from up the yards came in. She was a puny little thing and she wanted to buy a packet of cigarettes. 'I'm not selling you cigarettes for your mother,' she said. 'And you can go and tell her that. She's having a baby and she's not getting any Woodbines from here.' I don't know how Mrs Royal knew they were for her mother. Or whether the little girl then got them from another shop, but Beatty's mother had her principles. If everyone had done the same as her, that woman wouldn't have been able to smoke. And how did she find tuppence? Even though she was probably as poor as a church mouse and having another baby, she could still find tuppence for a packet of cigarettes.

One of us kids fetched the bread from my grandfather's bakery. My grandfather had married again when grandmother died, and my stepgrandmother was always there when I went, pottering in and out of the bakery office. (I didn't know my real grandmother, Elizabeth Varney. She died before I was born. She must have been illiterate,

My Stepgrandmother

'cause she only put a cross when she was married.) Grandfather's second wife was a tiny, little woman, and very inoffensive. I can't remember ever kissing her or loving her. I can't even remember having a conversation with her. But what I do remember is her singing: 'I want a piece of P-A-P-E-R to go across the yard?' I used to think, whatever's that old lady singing about? Grandfather might have had a big house, but they still didn't have a toilet inside. So my stepgrandmother had to go across the yard to the toilet just like we did. But she wasn't going to have no newspaper like we had. She used to use this lovely tissue what they wrapped bread in. At my house, we used newspaper, so we all had print on our bottoms. We'd cut it up in pieces, put them on a string and hang the string on a big nail.

One day I stopped off Woolworth's on Orford Place before I got the bread. It was opposite a place where they used to shoe all the horses. Everything was sixpence in Woolworths in them days. This particular day, I went to the counter with all the wedding rings. Oh, they were lovely. I kept fitting them on, putting them back, walking round the store. I wanted a wedding ring on my hand, 'cause I wanted to be a mother. I must have went round that counter six times, maybe more. And then suddenly I came out. I wanted a ring so bad, but I never stole. I'm glad I didn't.

Woolworths, Orford Place

**St Stephen's Street c. 1920 where Ethel cycled among the tram lines
with 'five loaves of bread in the pillow slip' on her back.**

Usually, I walked to the bakery. When I got to St Stephen's Street,
I used to run beside the tram. I used to try and beat it. Of course, I
never could, but I used to keep up with it. Sometimes I'd get home
from school a bit late and Mother wanted the bread for tea. So I'd say:
'Mother, can I have a bike?' And I'd craze her and craze her. And if
she'd got the money she'd say: 'Oh, go on then.' And she'd give me
tuppence. I'd rent a bike from a lady that lived between us and Silver
Street. I can't think of her name. I think her husband worked at the
brewery. She had several children. They had six or seven bikes, which
was quite a thing in them days. Not very good bikes, of course, but
they were roadworthy. She charged tuppence for half an hour, so I had
to get up there and back in half an hour, didn't I? I used to chase down
St Stephen's Street. There was all tram lines and trams coming. No
cars, of course not, but horses and carts. Five loaves of bread in the
pillow slip on my back, and riding with one hand. There was all

Castle Meadow, and Tombland.[78] And I had to go through Bank Plain at the back of the cathedral and then over the bridge and into Barrack Street and then to Cavalry Street. I'd give Mother the bread, the five loaves, so she could get on cutting. Poor old dear. She must have spent all her life cutting bread. Then I'd take the bike back. I'd just get to the lady's gate and throw the bike in, and run off. That was cheating really. But I didn't have no more money and I knew Mother didn't. I can see myself now - opening that gate and slinging the bike in. Because, if the woman saw me, it might be another penny.

Lipton's was a lovely place when I was a little girl, all fancy white tiling at the door. That was where Mother sometimes got her margarine and her eggs. I think they had butter, but us kids never saw that. You went in and there was a big marble counter. And they had a big plate with a huge block of margarine. I think Mother used to have three or four pounds a week. They used to cut a great lump off and get it on this slab. I used to love watching that. Then they'd cut it small in pounds and put each piece between these wood things with a rose pattern on. They were like two ping-pong things, but not quite so big. They used to clap them together and when they'd finished, you had a flower impression on top of the margarine. So when you got it and took it home that looked pretty, and when you put it on the table, it'd be fancy. We used to love that. Of course, once you started cutting, the flower go. Marge didn't stay in my house long.

After Mother got out of Mrs Howlett's clutches, she went to the Co-op every week for her shopping. It was a posh shop in them days. She went there on the tram. Sometimes, fat little Sally what lived

---

[78] Castle Meadow and Tombland are names of streets in the Norwich city centre.

near us would come round. 'Do y'ear Edwards', she'd say, 'they got some really nice stuff at that Co-op this week. You'd better get up there.' Sally was a lovely lady. As round as she was tall. She used to come to ours and talk to Mother. I think she used to borrow sugar now and again. Sometimes she'd get things for Mother if she was going up the city and if Mother couldn't get to the Co-op to get her dividends,[79] she'd give Alice something for doing it. And then when she got the money, she'd give us something for sweets.

Mother got her material from Price's. You went in there and there was a mature lady in black, with some nice little earrings on. She'd be always walking about the shop, to see that the assistants were doing their job right. You went to the assistant and paid your money. That would perhaps be a couple of shillings you'd spend. Well, that might be one and eleven pence three farthings. There were these overhead wires that went all round the shop, and a thing like a big eggcup that went along them. It used to fascinate me. The assistant opened it and put your money in it. Then she whizzed it along the wire thing up to the cashier. You could see her at her desk. She'd undo the egg cup, put your change in it and send it back. If that was only a farthing, a packet of pins or needles would come back in the egg cup. You didn't have no option. I suppose they couldn't be giving farthings out all the time. And we used to like pins and needles. They were all handy.

The chemist in Barrack Street was a little man. He looked like a professor. As you opened the door of his shop, you could smell all the beautiful things. He used to sell three slabs of soap in a lovely box, but he must have sold them separate as well, because he sometimes had an

---

[79] See footnote on p. 51

Burrage's Fish Shop in Barrack Street

Price's Department Store

empty box. I used to say to my friends: 'Come on. Let's go and ask that man if he's got any boxes.' And if he had one, he'd give you one. Beautiful they were. Smelt lovely. One day, we went in and he said: 'Can any of you sing?' They all say: 'Oh, she can. She can sing lovely.' And I can remember singing down this horn that recorded. I sang 'Romany Rose', and I giggled through it, 'cause they were looking at me. I heard it after. I sung lovely, but I could hear myself giggle in the middle of it. He said: 'You've got a lovely voice. He was the one what told me about his friend, Madame someone, what had a singing and dancing troupe.

Chamberlin, Sons & Co. c.1869

There were some lovely shops up the city in those days. Chamberlin's was the one on the market place on the corner, where Tesco's now is. That was a posh shop. The manageress was standing in the foyer when you went in. She stood there in a long black frock and earrings and nice pearls. Sometimes she'd walk about, but most often she'd be standing at the door to see people coming in. Butcher's in Swan Lane was another lovely shop. You could get anything there. The ladies in there what served you, they were all first class people.

Lyons, the tea place, was opposite the city hall. I used to go there when I was about eighteen. Oh that was beautiful. That was a shop where they served cakes, but if you wanted to go to the restaurant then you went up the stairs. All lovely tables with white table cloths. The people what served you had little white hats and black dresses. And pretty white pinafores what went over their shoulders and crossed at the back. All lace, nothing but lace, like the servants on Unthank Road used to wear. And nice black shoes and black stockings. Lovely ladies they were. They were elegant, and they used to serve you beautifully. The cakes were delicious. And that was about sixpence for a cup of tea. It was really something to go in Lyons. You felt you were with the gentry.

⁂

There was a shrimp man what used to come round the houses. He had a barrow and great big baskets full of winkles and shrimps and cockles. He wore an apron, all stripes, navy and white, and a big coat and big old boots. He didn't dress very good. My sister Nelly told me that when the shrimp man came she hated me. He'd always put a few shrimps in my little apron just for me, but he never give her any. The baby was the favourite in them days.

Mother let us choose what we wanted – shrimps or winkles – but we couldn't have both. She would get the table set and put them out on plates. And she'd give us all a pin to stick in the winkles and pull them out of their shell. We loved them but, the thing of it was, we'd all get up to the table and start counting. And then we all used to argue about how many we got. One of my brothers would say: 'I only got six'. And Mother, instead of counting out the right amount, she'd throw three or four on his plate. And then another one would say: 'Well, now he got more than me.' If Father had been there, there wouldn't have been none of that. But when Mother was on her own, that was what she had to contend with.

The vegetable lady was a character. A real country person, tall and thin with a long, black skirt, black lace-up boots, and an old sack around her. She had her black hair in a bun on the top, covered with a scarf, and she wore earrings. Big gold ones. She looked more like a Gypsy lady really, but I don't think she was. Mother had a little friendship with her. She used to run on talking. 'Yes,' she say, 'my brother and my sister-in-law, he's a mean-un and she's a mean-un.' I used to love to hear her say that and I'd mimic her when the others come home from work. She drove a horse and cart and she must have come miles, 'cause there weren't no country where we were. She was a tough old girl. She carried the big sacks of potatoes on her back. I suppose she had cows, 'cause she used to bring best butter. It was a lovely gold colour. That must have been the real thing. Mother used to buy one lot a week. I seen her get a couple of rounds of bread, spread it with butter, and sprinkle it with salt. Then she'd sit and enjoy it. I don't know whether she give it out much.

The milkman used to come round on a donkey. He had a little cart with two wheels at the back. And he used to have these big urns. They didn't have no bottles in them days. Mother went out with a jug, or a couple of jugs, but we didn't have too much milk. She couldn't afford it. The bread man used to come in an open cart with a horse at the front. Clean sacks and the bread just slung in. No cut bread at all. Of course, we used to get our bread from our grandfather.

A Norwich baker's cart of 1939

When we started having gas, we used to have a man come round to empty the meter. That was a treat in itself. We looked forward to it for a couple of months. 'Mother, when is the gas man coming?' we'd keep asking. Then one day we'd come home and Mother would say: 'He's been.' She must have got a good bit back, 'cause she put a lot in, with all the cooking she done.[80] She'd give us a ha'penny and keep the rest in her pocket. The poor man what emptied the meters must have been loaded. Carrying all them coppers round with him.

My mother was a lovely lady and she loved everybody, but she was absolutely petrified of Gypsies.[81] Years ago them old Gypsies did use

[80] For some reason, meters were set to take more money than was required to meet the cost of the gas consumed. The meter man's coming was looked forward to because the rebate he would provide was a small, but in those days significant, amount of cash.

[81] The Gypsies in Ethel's day were an ethnically more distinct group than the 'travellers' of today. They were part of the swarthy-skinned *Roma* family, descendants of a people who some 600 years ago were expelled from Northern India. After a period in Persia, they crossed into South Eastern Europe, and their descendants are still most numerous in that region today. The Roma's nomadic lifestyle took them all over the Continent, including into Britain. Those that visited Ethel's home would have spoken their own language and would have moved about the country in their distinctive horse-drawn wagons. More than anything else, it was the Roma's beliefs in the supernatural – the evil eye, talismans and lucky charms – that scared people like Ethel's mother.

to put spells on people, and I think Mother was frightened that they might put one on our family. People were a bit superstitious, and they probably thought on it so much that it really happened. Gypsies then were really Gypsies. They had black braids and big gold earrings dangling, and a red handkerchief on their heads. They came round with a big basket on their arm, with all these paper flowers and lace and dusters. I didn't know about dusters when I was little. We never had one, only the rags what Mother rent up. The Gypsy women used to bring little charms and say they would bring you luck and all that. If Mother saw them coming, she'd hide up on the stairs. But if she was in the kitchen and they come, she couldn't run away. So she used to say: 'I haven't got nothing and I don't want nothing, but I'll give you a cup of sugar or a bit of marge or cheese.' She never ever let them go away without something.

Gypsies on Ridlington Common

10. Christmas and other Special Days

Me and all the other kids in the street had a thing about Christmas. We'd be praying that Christmas would come soon, 'cause we knew that on Christmas Eve, Santa was going to bring us something, something that had to last us the whole year, 'cause we never got toys in between. Or even treats, for that matter. So, weeks before Christmas, we'd be asking each other: 'What do you think you're going to get?' The waiting was terrible, but the glory of it was, when you did put your hand in that stocking on Christmas morning, it was all for you. That bar of chocolate was your bar of chocolate. That orange was yours. You didn't have to share any of it.

Weeks before Christmas, I'd say: 'Mother, when you going to make the ginger wine?'[82] And she'd say: 'Oh it won't be long now.' First, she gathered a lot of bottles and cleaned them all out, so they were all shiny and good. And then she got corks to put in them. She made the wine in this big bowl what had a jug with it. That was a lovely china one with a silver rim round, what she used to bath all the babies in. But, of course, I was the last one, so there was no more of that. The bowl had to be washed and scalded out. Then she'd set all the bottles out on the table and fill them up from the jug. When they were cool, she put all the corks in. She done loads of bottles, and she always made a taster for us. Hot, I remember. Cor, that was lovely.

[82] Ethel's mother would have made the ginger wine by boiling up water, sugar, lemon zest and bruised ginger and then adding yeast to the mixture when it had cooled down to about blood heat. She may have added some lemon juice and raisins later. The mixture would have fermented sufficiently for drinking after about three weeks.

She'd keep the wine a couple or three weeks. And you could really smell it.

A couple of weeks before Christmas, Mother would make the cakes. All this lemon peel and eggs and sultanas and almond nuts in the mixture. I used to nick an almond if I could. I can see them now in these lovely tins with greaseproof paper round. They were all her own tins, but of course, she couldn't cook 'em at home, 'cause she only had this little oven in the wall. She had to put the tins on trays, and take them down to the baker's office. My sisters used to help her carry them. Mother didn't marzipan her cakes. I don't think she could go to all that trouble, and it cost money to get the sugar and stuff. I can see them now, all lying on the table. A lovely golden brown. And she always used to make a taster, what she cut up before Christmas. About a week before Christmas, she would give a cake and a bottle of ginger wine to all the brothers and sisters what were married. She couldn't give nothing else. But what a beautiful present.

Mother made Christmas puddings. Just enough for us what were still at home. She boiled 'em in the old copper what she did the laundry in, but it was cleaned out first. She used to put silver three-penny bits in the puddings. Only a couple, 'cause, she didn't have the money to spare. If you were lucky enough to find it, you got to keep it. You didn't have to share it. We all wished we could find one, but I don't think I ever did. We had to help Mother clean the house for Christmas. For starters, we used to scrub the cupboards. And then all the pictures had to come down. We used to have to clean the backs with paraffin. They were all polished and put back. And the silver had to be cleaned. We didn't have much. I got two spoons now what my mother had. My brother brought one of them home from the war.

Mother and Father used to get our presents from Brenner's old bazaar in Magdalen Street. When they come home with them, they first took them in the living room. 'All you kids get in the front room,' they used to say. We never did find out where Mother hid them, so we never knew what we were going to have. Maybe she hid them in the cupboard in her room, 'cause in them days, you weren't allowed to go in your mother's room and touch things. You wouldn't even think about it. I remember her saying: 'Don't you come in my room without knocking. I say: 'What for, Mother?' She say: 'Well your father might be dressing.'

On Christmas Eve, the front room was got ready. The chairs were all round. The beer was up the corner, and a crate of stout and half ales. You wanted to go to bed and you didn't want to go to bed. You wanted to go, 'cause you were going to wake up the next morning with a stocking. But then you didn't want to go to bed, 'cause you couldn't sleep. You'd be awake most of the night, trying to fathom out what you got in your black stocking. Us kids what were at home we'd keep up until about ten o'clock. And if Father was out, Mother would say: 'Come on. I'm going to bed.' She used to love to go to bed, poor old dear. And she would say: 'Now Walter's going to come round in the night. So when I come and wake you, all run to the window quick.' That was my brother, Walter, the one that was with the Salvation Army. They used to come regular every Christmas in the early hours of the morning. 'Come on, Walter's outside,' Mother would say, and we'd run and look out of the window. They'd stand under the lamp outside ours, and they'd play a couple of tunes. Then Walter would shout out: 'Good morning, Mr and Mrs Edwards. Happy Christmas.' He used to speak so lovely. I don't know where he got his speaking from. I suppose he had the Lord with him and that was coming through his speech. When they'd finished, we'd scramble back into the cold bed.

We'd fall asleep in the end, but by six o'clock in the morning I'd be awake. I'd feel what I got, 'cause that'd still be dark. At the bottom of the stocking, there'd be an apple and an orange. We never had that the rest of the year unless we were ill. Then there'd be a few nuts and a little bar of chocolate in a khaki carton with a royal blue stripe. Always Caley's chocolate.[83] And then, beside the stocking, there'd be a present. No more than one, 'cause the brothers and sisters couldn't buy you nothing. They had a job to buy their own children something.[84] No, my brothers and sisters never bought me anything

[83] The formula for making milk chocolate bars was only discovered in 1876. Albert Caley saw the potential market. In 1883 he opened a factory in Norwich and soon became one of the biggest chocolate-producers in England. His chocolate was of excellent quality and he obtained warrants for providing several of his products to the royal family. A bar of Caley's 'Marching Chocolate' was frequently found in the British troops' kit bags during the Great War. Ethel worked at Caley's for a short time.

[84] Christmas time was very hard for the unemployed. Just before the Christmas that Ethel was six, the *Norwich Mercury* described the scene outside the Guildhall where a Council meeting was taking place about whether more funds could be made available to help the unemployed:

'On the one hand was Norwich Market Place in all its time-honoured Christmastime garb. There were the brilliantly lighted stalls laden with a wealth of holly and mistletoe with evergreens, with fat geese and juicy joints of beef. There were the vendors of toys and the vendors of sweets – just the old-time picture of happy prosperous Christmastides of old. But gathered round the old grey Guildhall was a little army of white-faced unemployed men and women in whose hearts was no Christmas cheer. Workless, hungry, they were facing the should-be glad season with bitter despair.

There was no good news from the meeting. Most of the crowd dispersed but some "younger and wilder spirits" rushed off down London Street and smashed windows of the grocer's (International Stores) and looted. Police arrived to stop trouble but [presumably in a spirit of seasonal good will] seem to have let the crowd escape with what they'd stolen.'

The accompanying editorial concluded that unless something was done '...the part of the nation which is workless, hungry and desperate will burst forth like a ravaging flood and make existence impossible for all.'

on my birthday or anything. Never even got a card. But what a wonderful thing Christmas morning was, when you might get some toy weighing scales for playing shop, or a doll, or a picture book. Only a small thing, but there was no need for any more. You'd have it with you all day. You wouldn't let it out of your sight. And the best thing was the brothers and sisters had something too, so you didn't have to share it. You'd play with it for weeks and weeks.

When we come downstairs on Christmas morning, the log fires would be blazing in the living room and the front room. We'd have a good breakfast. The older ones had a whole egg and a sausage and a fair bit of meat. For the rest of us, there'd be a bit of steak, half a sausage, half an egg and loads of gravy. And your half egg went into the gravy, so you could suck it up. Christmas day was the only day Father ever stopped in. He had a barrel of beer up the corner of the front room. And of course he had to keep testing it. He cooked the chicken in the oven in the wall. We didn't have a turkey. We never knew there was a turkey alive. Of course in them days there weren't no chicken-all-the-year-round like there is now. It was just an average chicken we'd have, one what Uncle Billy used to grudgingly give us. I don't know how we managed with all us lot. Father used to have a leg and mother dished it out as best she could. We all got a tiny bit. And then we used to have a huge lump of pork to go with it.

After dinner, Mother cleared the table, and my sisters washed up. Then a bit later, Mother would get this lovely big cloth out and put it on the table for tea. We'd be looking at the clock and I'd be thinking: 'Oh, they're all going to come down soon.' Poor old Mother, she used to cook all that dinner for us, and then she'd have the rest of them round for Christmas tea and supper. They'd all come, sons, daughters, husbands, wives, and all the grandchildren. I don't know however we all got in. Father would be sitting smoking his cigar, and the beer coming out of the barrel. The men had Father's beer and the women had their stout. Us kids used to have ginger wine. For tea, there was salmon, and salt beef. And crawfish, 'cause you could get some lovely crawfish for eleven pence. And when you opened the tin that was all proper fish. Like finger bits. Then, there were Mother's sausage rolls. And there'd be a penn'orth or two penn'orth of pickled onions in a glass. And buns and a bit of Christmas cake each.

I can't remember many Christmas trees, but you'd look out and see all the people's windows lit up. They didn't pull the blinds, so you could see in. We'd all sit around on chairs. I can't remember if we hired them from the pub or they brought them down from their flats. One Christmas, my sister Clara brought her piano. Her and her husband Claude wheeled it all the way down from Mousehold Street right into our front room. He locked it up when they went in the other room, but I got underneath it, and I started playing it, which was naughty. I was a little tear-away really. Later on, we'd sing all the lovely old songs. We'd go round in turn. You sang your song, and then everyone would join in with you. Rose's song was 'Charmaine', Hilda's was 'Arise Beloved' and mine was 'Romany Rose'. Our other favourite songs were:

> Just a song at twilight
> Land of hope and glory
> Lilly of Laguna
> She's my ladylove
> Pack up your troubles in your old kit bag
> Roses are blooming in Picardy
> When I leave the world behind

Smile awhile
Carolina Moon
Keep the home fires burning
By the Light of the Silvery Moon

And all the time, they were drinking and cracking nuts, and having a bit of orange. I can't ever remember a box of chocolates coming out. No, they weren't handing round chocolates. They couldn't afford them. But we had loads of nuts. Brazil nuts, walnuts, peanuts. And oranges. Mother used to get forty at Kay's. Forty oranges for a shilling. They'd all be cut up on these big serving plates. It was all quarters. The only time we ever had a whole orange was the one what we had in our stocking. We used to peel the skin off. Then we used to turn them the other way round and cut them like we had false teeth. We'd put them in our mouths, and keep talking. Later, we used to have tongue for supper. We only ever had it at Christmas. And of course Mother had pressed it herself. She'd have her white apron on and she'd sit there, cutting it up. And the girls would put it on plates with the bread and butter. It weren't just a sandwich.

Walter went to the citadel at Christmas, but about nine o'clock in the evening he used to come home. He'd say hello and they'd all be smoking and drinking and overeating. He'd have a nice sandwich of mother's salt beef, and a lemonade or something, just to be sociable. He'd sit with us for a little while, but he couldn't bring himself to stay, 'cause it wasn't his cup of tea. 'Goodnight all,' he'd say, and he'd go up to bed. He couldn't have slept with all that racket going on, but he didn't want to be in that atmosphere all the while. I mean they weren't bad people. They were just enjoying themselves.

None of them didn't go back to their homes that night. The women and children went to bed about ten o'clock. They got into whatever beds they could up there. Me and Nelly used to get in with Mother. And the others were all top and tailing. The men and the boys kept the fire going downstairs, and stayed up the whole night playing cards. The next morning I got to the top of the stairs and there was this aroma of cigars, beer, orange peel and nuts coming up. There were nutshells all over the floor downstairs. Poor old Mother. She had to give everyone breakfast. Then they'd all disperse. Boxing Day was Father's day, and he'd be out the whole day.

❖

On Valentine's Day, kids done naughty things. They used to tie two front door handles together, and then run away and hide. And when the people come to the doors, they couldn't open them. Other times, they'd open the door, and old tins would fall on their heads. And we used to leave parcels on the doorsteps. We'd bang on the door and run away. They'd all be wrapped up beautiful. But anything nasty, we'd put inside. Old salmon tins, stale fish heads, manure, dogs' mess. Oh yes. And they had to open it, 'cause they didn't know if it was the real thing. But then they'd get mad. They'd shout and swear, and throw it in the street. But they didn't know who you were, 'cause you'd be hiding in a doorway. That was a naughty thing really. The boys were always the worst offenders. I can't say I ever done it, but I was with them, and so I was as bad as them what done it.

❖

Easter was nice, when I was a little girl. I don't remember ever having Easter eggs, but on Good Friday, my brothers used to go out selling hot cross buns. Mother would give them a clean tray and fit them up with a lovely clean cloth, and they'd be out at six o'clock in the morning. All the way round, you could hear: 'Hot cross buns, hot cross buns, one a penny, two a penny hot cross buns.' Mother always used to buy some. Of course, you didn't have one each. People would buy two or three, and cut them in halves or quarters. Me and Nelly had new clothes at Easter. Mother bought us shoes, and a hat from Price's. A little straw hat with all flowers, sometimes orange and yellow daisies, sometimes pretty little rosebuds. I used to go to my step-grandma's on Easter morning. And I loved looking at myself in my lovely Easter hat and shoes in all the shop windows. Sometimes I got black patent shoes. I can remember once I had a penny from my Aunt Rose. But I was stood near a drain and I let my penny down. Two men come past and they say: 'What you crying for?' I say: I lost my penny.' So they give me some. They must have been men in good jobs, I should think. I ended up with tuppence or threepence.

⌖

I loved Empire Day. In every household the children looked lovely, even the boys. They had nice socks on, and little white shirts, and the girls had white dresses, and perhaps we'd have a pink sash. At school, they picked a queen. She sat on this big thing with wheels and she carried a Rule-Britannia-thing. Ooh I wanted to be that, but I never was picked. We were always dressed clean, but there were some in the school that were only children, what had better clothes than me, and one of them would be Britannia. She was dressed up in the red, white and blue, and the crown on her head. And they pushed her in on these wheels. Then we all used to sing and dance round the maypole. The Lord Mayor would come and give us a little chat. Then he said: 'Boys and girls, you can have the rest of the day off.' And we used to scream out: 'Hurray'. [85]

Empire Day celebrations at Nelson Street School, Norwich

✥

Nearly every kid in the street had a turnip at Halloween. The others had Swedes, which were bigger. We cut out faces in them, with a nose, a mouth and teeth. And then we used to eat the raw turnip and swede. That was a treat. On Halloween night, we put a candle in the turnip lantern and we walked round trying to frighten one another. We loved walking around in the dark.

✥

On Bonfire Night, they used to have a big bonfire on Mousehold. I don't think anyone had one in the garden. They didn't have much to

[85] The log book for Ethel's school for 24 May 1924 noted: 'To celebrate Empire Day, the schools were visited in the afternoon by the Deputy Mayor, Mr G.H. Morse, Miss Morse, Mr & Mrs R.F. Betts and other friends; at 2.30 the three schools assembled in infants' playground for a programme of songs, dances etc.' The entry for 1925 records 'an inspiring address' from the Lord Mayor. The school also celebrated Trafalgar Day. On 24 October 1918, 'being the anniversary of the Battle of Trafalgar, all the children were assembled and stories were told of the Battle and also incidents in the life of Nelson, afterwards a sand-tray model of the battle was made by the children'.

burn really, but they used to look around and find a lot of old truck. There were fireworks. What little we had, we took to share. There were Catherine Wheels, Roman Candles, and Rockets. They didn't hurt you. There weren't none of these horrendous-noise ones what they do now. And I can always remember having sparklers. They were a ha'penny a packet.

The Tram

The men didn't have a week's holiday when I was growing up. But they musta had Monday and Tuesday for August bank holiday. Monday was Father's day out, but he always kept the Tuesday for our day trip to Yarmouth. The night before we went, I couldn't sleep. 'Is it time to get up?' I'd keep asking. I was all on hot bricks, waiting for Mother to give us something to eat and get us ready. She took one or two things in her bag what we could eat, and this 'ere little toilet pot. And we all had our pail and spade. That was only a little way from Kett's Hill to Thorpe Station, but we went on this lovely tram. Oh, that was really, really a treat. We used to love to go up the stairs, 'cause it was all open on top. Of course, if it rained we got soaking wet. I can see the old tram driver at the front now, with his wheel going one way and then another, and his great old navy coat and his black peak cap with red round it.

When we got to the railway station, we were raring to go. We ran onto the platform, while Mother got the tickets. Then she came and got us on the train and sorted us out. We all behaved ourselves. I can remember one time there was a man sitting near us on the train. And my father said: 'Would you like to sing, Ethel?' I said: 'Oooh no!' And the man said: 'Oooh, do she sing?' I must have been very tiny and my father say: 'Yeh'. So I sung 'Romany Rose'. And the man

The Yarmouth Beach Express

gave me sixpence. When we got to Yarmouth we got off the train and walked over the bridge. Mother and Father used to call in the big pub on the right as you left the station. Father had his half pint and Mother had a stout. They wouldn't be there for long. It was just their little treat. They'd get a stone bottle o' pop for us to share.

On the way to the seafront, Mother went into a baker's shop and got two lovely crusty long loaves. And she'd buy some ham to go with them. She brought the marge from home. When we got to the beach, she spread the tablecloth on the sand, and Father and all us children sat round. I can see her now, sitting there, prim and proper in a black coat over her black skirt, and a hat. Always a black hat, big brimmed and tall. And my father, very smart in his trilby, his cheat and his grey tweed suit and buttonhole. Mother cut the bread and made the ham sandwiches. She and Father would have a cuppa tea, which was tuppence. And she got us an orange drink between us. Then we'd go in the sea. Mother used to sit right near, so she could keep an eye on us. The sea would come over your feet and then that would draw away. You felt you were flying. She'd give us a fair amount of time there on the beach. We didn't have no donkey ride, 'cause she couldn't afford to pay for us. But after we'd been there quite a while, we'd all go up from the beach and get on an open landau. That was our special treat. It took us right to the Pleasure Beach,[86] but we didn't go round the fair. Mother probably thought, they can't go on nothing, so no good letting them go in. And then we'd have this lovely open landau to take us back.

When it was time to go home, we'd walk to the station. There was no toilets on the trains in them days. So, going there and coming back this little pot was always available. Mother wouldn't have us uncomfortable, and she made sure we didn't wet ourselves. I think we all had a little tinkle in it, because we were drinking this lovely drink what we weren't used to. Then Mother would throw it out the window. We were a bit tired when we got home, but that day was really, really a lovely treat. It was like Christmas all again.

[86] The Pleasure Beach was the funfair at the end of the seaside promenade in Great Yarmouth.

11. Being Sick

Mother put us all in an insurance scheme for a penny a week when I was a bigger girl, so we could go to the doctor's if we were really ill. If you were insured, you could go to a place up near the market. It was called The Institute, and it was full of medicines.[87] You gave them your prescription and then you'd sit round on forms, waiting. When they called your name you'd have to go up to get your medicine through a little door. And every time they opened it to give someone their prescription, this aroma used to come through. Oh, lovely smells they were. Different medicines, I suppose. But if you weren't insured, you couldn't go there.

When we were little, doctors weren't seen hardly. No. People couldn't afford them. There was hospitals, but you had to be nearly dead for them to take you in. If you didn't have a doctor you could go to Smith's, the pharmacy in Magdalen Street. When you opened that door, and walked in, you could see all these big, coloured bottles. It used to smell beautiful, and if you had the money, they would make up whatever medicines you asked for. So people would go and get what

[87] Those members of Ethel's family in full-time work would have been insured for very basic medical care under Lloyd George's national insurance scheme enacted in 1911. However, this insurance did not cover dependents. Thus, if Ethel's mother or any of her children needed medical assistance, they would have to arrange private insurance, probably with a local doctor's practice, or pay for the treatment as needed. Since they had no room in the household budget to afford this, they, like all women and children in poor families, went without medical treatment even when it was critically needed. Understandably, the introduction of a comprehensive National Health Service after the Second World War was the most welcomed of all the welfare provisions introduced by the new Labour Government.

they thought was alright. But of course, you didn't always know what you needed. That's why I think a lot of 'em died. [88]

In them days, there was no such thing as going to the hospital when you had a baby. But can you imagine having a baby with all them children round? When my sisters had babies, they relied on a midwife or a woman what lived near. I don't think any of them were really that qualified. They were just little old women who could deal with it. The basin what they bathed the baby in was the one we made the ginger wine in at Christmas. After you'd had the baby, the neighbours would help out. They'd do a bit of washing, or they'd bring you a little something to eat.

We were some of the fortunate ones. Mother had them lovely standards, and she had the sense to know how to look after us. Every Friday night, she used to dish us out some syrup of figs. You didn't have to be ill. It was just to keep your bowels regular and your blood all clean. [89] When she couldn't afford the syrup of figs, we used to have the sennapods. She did them in a big jug, like cold tea with no sugar in. And then sometimes we had Epsom salts which were terrible.

[88] At this time the newspapers were full of advertising for self-medication wonder cures. Ads for Dr William's pink pills ('Can't get warm? – some signs of thin blood') would vie for attention with Dr Cassell's tablets ('Failure of the nerves – utterly helpless for six years, yet cured by Dr Cassell's tablets') Even food adverts targeted health concerns. The locally made Mackintosh's toffee was advertised as 'The toffee that is all food'. And not drinking Bovril was claimed to be the reason 'Why women age quickly.'

[89] It was only during the later part of the 20th century that people became less concerned about regular bowel movements. During Ethel's childhood parents were obsessed with this subject and of the crucial need for a good weekly 'clean out'. The horror of the Friday night administration of senna pods and other laxatives turns up frequently in oral histories. The obsession probably dates back to times when doctors believed that the best way to cure patients was to purge the 'foul humours' causing the disease. This led them to prescribe laxatives freely, not only to cure but also to prevent illnesses.

She'd give you a little cup and you'd have to drink it. It was like swallowing little bits of glass. They was supposed to clean your blood.

We were pretty healthy really, but with such a big family, there was always one of us ill. And when you were sick, that was a torture. Terrible pains you'd have. Mother would give us Tincture Rhubarb.[90] She bought it at Mrs Howlett's. She used to have it in glass jars. That wasn't nothing to do with making you go to the toilet. Well, that did make you go, but it was for your illness. It sweated you. You could smell it. Ugh! And there was always a lot of trouble, 'cause you didn't want to have it and so you'd move your head when mother was trying to give it you. Then, she'd give you a clip over the ear, even though you were ill. Oh, it was vile. But it did do us good. Then there was something like ipecacuanha wine[91] they used to give you. That was if you were really, really ill. That was vile an' all. But what else could they do, poor things? And a lot of them women in them days were wonderful, 'cause they did usually get you better in the end.

I used to have styners[92] a lot. That was a common thing, and a lot of kids had them. I don't know why I did, 'cause we had good food. They come up like little red balls on your eyelid, and then go yellow. We used to say: 'I've got a styner on my eye, mother.' And she'd bathe it, 'cause it had to burst. We didn't have eyewash. She'd bathe it with

---

[90] Tincture of rhubarb was widely used as an all-purpose medicine. In large doses, it had a laxative effect, while in smaller doses it had the opposite effect and was used to combat diarrhoea. It can still be bought today in herbal remedy shops.

[91] Ipecacuanha wine was made from ipecac, the dried root of the ipecacuanha plant. It was used to ease coughs and asthmatic attacks and, in larger doses, it induced vomiting. Ipecac is still used as a powerful emetic today and is administered to those who have swallowed poisons.

[92] styes

boracic lint. Get a saucer and put the boracic crystals in some really hot water. Today they give you antibiotics and they clear up quick. But then, you'd just have to wait till it wanted to finish. Bathin' it, bustin' it, bathin' it, and bustin' it. Sometimes it come again, or maybe it didn't go away at all. You could have two or three all at once.

I had ringworm once. My sister Clara's daughter May had a hat. A lovely bonnet it was, pale blue velvet and pink flowers. And I said to her: 'Can I borrow it?' She said: 'No, but you can fit it on if you like.' So I wore it for nearly a day when I was up at hers. My sister said nothing. But May must have had the ringworm, and I got it from her. I might have been able to get away with it for a minute, but not wearing the hat all that time. They were like rings. They started like a little marble and then they got bigger and bigger. And your hair, it just come off. Mother used to put iodine on. My poor sister Nelly, she had 'em terrible. We both had one what was right in the middle of our head, but Nelly had a lot of sores come out with it too. She couldn't sleep, poor girl. Screaming in the night. And she said: 'It was you what wore her bonnet. You shouldn't have had it on.' Poor old mother had to get us right again. That was what happened in our house, but I suppose lots of people had them.

Tonsillitis, I used to have that a lot when I was a kid. And if you got tonsillitis in them days, you were really ill. Mother used to just let us gargle with some salt water. But, when your throat was sore, it was a bit of a job. And of course, you didn't have straws at that time of day. If you'd had straws, you could have got a little liquid down. And you couldn't eat nothing. Mother would go out and get us an orange and we'd suck it. That was a treat. You only got an orange at Christmas, or if you were ill.

One of us got the mumps, and we all caught it 'cause we all slept together.[93] Mother used to say: 'Come on, all get it and let's get it over with.' Ooh, that was terrible. There were great lumps under your neck. You couldn't move it one way or the other. And then your jaws all swelled up. Horrible pain. Horrible medicine. And one thing what Mother did for you, which she thought was good. She got a great lump of fat – you know, from the pig – and she put it on your throat. A big lump of pork fat round your neck. She then put a big piece of flannelette round it and put a pin in, so it kept on. It was on for a few days, the same bit, 'cause Mother couldn't afford to keep buying more. Oh, I hated it. That used to stink. I don't know what that was supposed to do. When you think about it, it probably didn't do anything.

Poor Mother. One time, she got two great big boils on her behind, and of course, she couldn't afford to go to the doctors. Me, little nosy parker, I musta went up and had a look. Great big'uns they were. With pus in 'em. Every night she used to go upstairs with Father after tea and he had to put a hot poultice on them. Boiling water and a bit o' lint. He had to keep putting it on and pressing to try and get the pus out. I could hear her moaning. 'Ohhh,' she used to cry. Poor dear. I was only a little girl and I used to cry when I heard her crying.

---

[93] Ethel and her siblings were lucky in avoiding the serious contagious illnesses – such as scarlet fever, diphtheria, and phthisis (tuberculosis) – that were endemic in the Norwich of her childhood. Those infected could expect stays of several weeks in the Isolation Hospital. In November 1924, Miss Trollope, a teacher at Ethel's school caught diphtheria from one of the pupils and was sent to the isolation hospital where she remained for three months. Diphtheria, an acute respiratory disease, was of particular concern because it often led to severe heart and nervous system complications. Two girls who were at school with Ethel – Gladys Brown and Ina Ward – both aged 10, died of it in 1923. Nation-wide immunization began in the 1940s and the annual national death toll plummeted from 2,480 in 1940 to 37 in 1957 and zero in most years over the past three decades.

When mother had twist of the bowels,[94] she was so bad that the Norfolk and Norwich hospital took her in. Not once – three times. They didn't allow children in hospitals in them days, so when they all went to see her, I had to go down to my brother Albert's. I was broken-hearted. I lay on this horse-hair settee, the tears and the prickles all sticking to my face. After they left the hospital, they all got together and had a drink. And then they come back to Albert's house and pick me up. They let me go and see her about the third day. I looked at her through a big window at the front of the hospital. She waved to me. But I couldn't go and kiss her, so I was ever so sad. And then when she come home, she got stuck into work straight away, didn't she?

One time, Edie was playing in this cold water outside and she did something to her arm. It got so cold, that she couldn't use it at all. So Mother took her to the hospital. And they said: 'Oh she'll never get no feeling back in that arm. Just let's cut it off.' But Mother said: 'No. If that's not going to do no harm, let it hang on. I want my little daughter to have her arm. What matter if it's just hanging there? It's better than no arm.' They tried and tried, but they couldn't do nothing with it. It just wouldn't move. Then, a few months later, she was playing with my brothers one day. One of them must have upset her, 'cause she got this arm and hit him with it. They shout: 'Mother! Mother! Edie's arm's all right!' Well, that was a godsend really, a

---

[94] The human intestine is several metres long looped around within the abdomen. Occasionally, one of these loops of bowel twists on itself blocking the movement of food through the digestion process. The bowel squeezes to overcome the obstruction, causing pain, swelling, and vomiting. Generally, surgery is required to unblock the stoppage. Without it, the condition leads to gangrene of the bowel wall, toxins seeping into the bloodstream and death. Maurice Gibb of the rock group the Bee Gees succumbed to the complications of a twisted bowel in 2003.

blessing from the Lord, 'cause she done a lot of hard work in her lifetime.

Brother Frank was a lovely man. He lost a leg he did. Not in the war. He didn't even go to war. When they were little, my brothers couldn't afford to go in the swimming pool, so they used to go down the Quay side, and swim in the river. And one time, Frank got a germ in the top of his leg. That was like a big football at the top of his leg, all yellow pus and green. It was so horrible that Mother had to get Dr Hepburn to come and deal with it. But it was ages and ages getting right. They got it reasonably well in the end, and they thought it had cleared up. But after a few years, when he was a young man, this leg started to play up and he had to have it off. He had a wooden one, and he had to walk with a stick, but no one would ever know he only had one leg.

I got runned over once and I had to go to the hospital. Ooh it was terrible. We were playing out in the street. There were about seven of us. And this day we were playing touch-and-run. The road was clear when we looked, but I don't think we were paying a lot of attention. You see, we didn't have to worry about no motor cars in them days. Well, this girl touched me. I started running across the road, and I never heard the bike. And I didn't see this teacher riding down the hill. I don't suppose that the poor man see me until he was nearly on top of me. He hit me, and I was flung on the edge of the path. I cut all my chin. Ooh, it all hung out. It was horrible. I had to go to hospital. We went on the tram. But, oh they were stern. You mustn't speak a word. I felt every stitch going in. And every time I spoke, it dragged on the stitches. I must have went up to the hospital for a month. But every time I went, they just ripped the scab off with tweezers, and it all started bleeding again. I think in the end, Mother bathed it off and it didn't come back no more. So it was a long job, this chin business. I've still got the scar.

'I hope you fall off the scaffold and break your neck.' Sometimes Mother used to say that to Father when she got angry with him. Then one day he didn't come home, 'cause he'd fell off the scaffold. They took him to hospital and he was plastered up. Front and back. It was a sticky plaster. Not the sort what you can break off. Father was a long time getting right, but when he did get right, they didn't pull the plaster off in the hospital. Mother couldn't do it, so he went upstairs with my brothers. He was like a hairy monkey. His back and body was full of hairs, absolutely full. We heard him scream when they pulled it off.

I dreaded going to the dentist. We all used to have toothache, and I'd be nights up, crying, waking Mother up. She'd say: 'We'll have to take you to the dentist.' 'No,' I said. 'I don't want to go.' They sat you in a chair and you shook like a leaf. They put this blue stuff on your tooth before they pull it out, but you could still feel it. You actually felt it come out. Of course, you cried. But you'd already cried for two or three nights before you went, which was silly. You might as well have went in the beginning, 'cause you had to go in the finish.

Part Two

FROM MY TEENS TO MY WEDDING

Ethel with a Marcel wave

12. Reaching my Teens

When I was thirteen I started going up the city with Maudie on Sunday and Wednesday evenings. I shouldn't have done. But I was mature for my age, and I never done nothing wrong. Mother didn't know and Father didn't know, 'cause we never said nothing. Oh no, I wouldn't tell Mother. She'd have had a fit. I remember one day we were going to the museum with the school. And of course, as kids, we all had to walk in line. And I was afraid that someone what I'd seen on the Prince of Wales Road in the evening would see me and know that I was still at school. So I kept my head down all the while.

I knew about kissing when I was thirteen. That was nice. But other than that, I never knew nothing. I remember, a girl at school saying: 'I know something rude about your mother and father.' And I say: 'What do you know about my mother and father?' 'They had to do rude before they had their seventeenth child.' Well, I was indignant. My mother and father wouldn't do anything like that. I went home and told Mother. And she said: 'Oh, don't you let your father hear you say anything like that.' So I went back to this girl and told her she was a liar.

One day when I was at school, I saw this blood, and I didn't know what it was. I didn't tell Mother, 'cause you didn't talk about things like that to your mother. But when my sister Rose come home, I tell her: 'There's all this blood.' She say: 'Oh you're having a period.' And she got me these things to use. I seen Mother make them up on the machine from toweling what she used to buy. And Rose say to me:

'You mustn't play with boys any more.' I thought what's that got to do with blood? What's she talking about? I honestly didn't know. I remember Billy's young lady, Edith, saying: 'If you're in any trouble, you let me know and I'll look after you.' Well, I didn't know what trouble I'd be in, 'cause I never thought of doing nothing wrong. Now I realise she must have meant if I went with a boy and got pregnant. But when I was thirteen, I never even knew anything like that existed.

Billy and Edith's wedding 1927
Ethel (second from left) and Nelly (far right) were bridesmaids

Father had a sister older than him, Aunt Ellen. She was a little old lady and she didn't have no teeth but one big'un down the bottom and one big'un up at the top. She was a widow, and she used to come to my mother's every Sunday for dinner and tea. Father would buy her and Mother a stout. Aunt Ellen liked her little bottle of drink. She had one son what was killed in the 1914 war and two other sons. They were in the war too, and sometime they come round ours with her on a Sunday.

Nelly and I did all the washing up on Sundays, and the wiping up and clearing away. Then sometimes her and I would go upstairs and have a little lay down. Well, one Sunday we were having a bit of sleep when we heard someone come upstairs. We were sleeping in just our petticoats and we were sort of aware that it wasn't the persons we were used to having upstairs. Then these two men came in the bedroom and sort of tried to get hold of us. I can't explain it, but it didn't feel right. Nelly was sick. I was sick. We both flew out of the bed. We jumped up and we put our dresses on. We didn't have no dressing gowns or anything like that. We come down stairs, and they come down. But never did we go upstairs anymore on a Sunday, 'cause we were too nervous they'd come up again. Mother, I suppose she thought that was all right. Two uncles coming up and saying hello.

⠀⠀⠀

When I started work, Mother used to give me a shilling a week for myself. So when I heard that you could go to the Corporation baths[95] and have a bath for tuppence, I said to her: 'Can I go?' 'Of course you can,' she say. 'You're getting a young woman now.' So Tilly and I, we both went. We paid our money to the lady there. She wore this big old apron and a blue dress. She looked a bit manly. At the time, I thought she were old, but they all looked old in them days. She went in and washed the bath out, and she wiped the toilet seat. And then she turned on the water. Whooosh. It came shooting in. Boiling water. You could hear it gushing. She let some cold water in. And then she

---

[95] Many towns and cities built public baths from the mid-nineteenth century onwards. They provided a cheap opportunity for poor people without bathroom facilities at home to take a bath and get themselves clean. They were part of the great Victorian effort to improve sanitary conditions and improve public health.

turned it off. You couldn't turn it on yourself. Oh no. I think she had a key to let in a certain amount. And I thought, ooh, this is posh. I went in the big old tin bath at home, but this was the first time I'd ever been in a proper bath. Lovely and warm. She let you stay in a good while, but if you were in a little longer than you should, she'd be banging on your door. She weren't going to let you be there all night.

After I got out of the bath, I pulled the plug out. The lady come in again, and washed it all down with some sort of bath-brick-looking stuff. Very hygienic. It was a lovely place to go, but it only lasted about four weeks. One day Tilly was in mine, and my father was there. He say to her: 'D'you go to the baths with Ethel?' And she say: 'Yes, and a man got a ladder and he looked at us.' I tell Father: 'That's not true.' 'Oh yes it is,' Tilly say. 'A man got a ladder and looked over the top at us.' I couldn't convince Father that the man didn't do it. Tuppence to go in. That was a lot of money. As though they'd let you pay that, and then let someone go and get a ladder and look over the top. But Tilly kept saying it. So Father wouldn't let me go no more. No. I can't understand him falling for that. Of course, he didn't know what the baths were like, 'cause he never went, did he? When he had a wash, he just stripped down. (He'd wash in the kitchen for his everyday wash and in his bedroom for an all-over wash.) If he'd had any sense and wanted to find out, he could have went down to see. They'd have thought he was crackers, wouldn't they? That was all Tilly's imagination. But why did she have to tell my father? Why couldn't she have told Mother?

13. Going to Work

I couldn't wait for the day I left school. My friend Maud, who lived opposite me, left in the August, 'cause she was a few months older than I was. So, there she was working, and I was still at school. That grieved me no end, 'cause she was my friend and I wanted to be like her. I don't remember where she was working, but when I left school, I started working at Batson and Webster's Boot and Shoe Operatives.[96]

My sister Rose had a friend what was a forewoman there and she got me the job. When they had the work, we had to work from seven till seven. We shouldn't have done 'cause we were only 14. We were kids. And we never had a Saturday morning off either. On Saturdays

---

[96] Traditionally, the production of textiles had been Norwich's most important industrial activity, but this shrunk rapidly in the 19th century with growing competition from the new mechanized mills elsewhere. From the latter part of the century, the boot and shoe industry took its place. There was already a well-developed leather industry in Norwich and a tradition of craftsmen making shoes in their homes. Taking advantage of this good supply of materials and skills and recently developed machinery, several boot and shoe factories began operations. Ethel refers to various types of work undertaken in the factories. The main stages of boot and shoe production were:

Clicking – cutting out the uppers.

Rough stuff cutting – cutting of all other materials for the shoe

Machining & upper closing – stitching together the uppers

Lasting – putting together the uppers, insoles, outsoles and stiffeners

Finishing – all edges trimmed, edges & heels inked & burnished

Treeing, cleaning & boxing

Many of the factories were old and crowded with poor heating and ventilation. Ethel describes the smells as being 'horrible'. Full-time employment was not guaranteed for all workers and when orders ran low many would be laid off.

When Ethel was a young woman, more than ten thousand people were employed in more than twenty boot and shoe factories in Norwich with a combined output of up to six million pairs of shoes per year.

Batson and Webster's where Ethel first worked was hit by a high incendiary bomb in a daytime raid by high-flying bombers during the Second World War. Some of Ethel's old colleagues may well have been among the casualties.

we used to go in from 8 till 12. So you can see, we done quite a few hours. Six shillings a week I got and tuppence an hour if I worked overtime. You give your Mother the pay packet in them days, and then she used to give you something back. I got a shilling, but then sometimes during the week Mother would give me some more. You see I was the last one, so I didn't do too bad.

My first day of work was a bit frightening. I was in a new world, and I felt very nervous. I saw all these people what I thought were very old. They were probably only eighteen or nineteen, but that was old to me, and they used to dress oldish in them days. The shoe room was full of horrible smells. And of course when you're young, your nose is very sensitive. My nostrils got full. Lemon smells, pear-drop smells, almond smells, solution smells, dressing smells, all coming from the different chemicals to clean, glue and polish the shoes. They all had a smell of their own. It used to be nauseating to begin with. You got used to it after a time, but it can't have been very good for you.

The men in the clicking room were the ones what used to cut out everything for the shoes. The uppers and the socks. The clickers wore plain white calico aprons. They were khaki when they first had them. But when their wives boiled them up, they then got right white. They had this leather bit on the front, 'cause I suppose that part wore out quickly. The people in the making room were the ones what put the shoes together. Then there were the sockers. They had to put the socks in the shoes before anyone could clean them. When I first started work, I ran about for the sockers. I were a little skivvy, really. I had to go up two flights of wooden stairs to get the socks from the clicking room. I was running up and down all day. If I went up there once, I went up a hundred times. I can remember this woman what was a socker. Her name was Ella, a spinster. She was very plain looking and she had her hair in a bun. Spinstery looking, you'd say. She wore an overall. Just an ordinary overall, what she used to tie at the back. 'Ethel, socks please.' That's all I got all day long. Her and another woman. All I could hear was them shouting. It got my back up a bit, but I suppose they had to shout, 'cause I weren't always near them. But the thing of it was I didn't like the tone in their voices. 'Ethel, Socks please.' I used to think: 'Oh, not again.' But I dursen't say no. I had to run. I brought an armful down at a time, but they'd use them up and then they'd want some more. I was up and down them stairs all day long, like a yoyo. And for six shillings a week.

Sometimes, I had to go up to the clicking room, when the men had already left off. When I was up there by myself, I used to like going on their board and cutting a bit of stuff out. Nothing to harm. I never done nothing to the work. But one time, I was really naughty. When the men went home they left their calico aprons on the boards.[97] And this one time when I was up there on my own, I suddenly see these apron strings. And I thought, oh I'll have all them off. I knew they couldn't do the aprons up without the strings, so I must have really meant it. I cut them all off. Oh it was terrible. Whatever made me do such a wicked thing? The next day when I went up, there they all stood. Their aprons undone instead of tied-up. They didn't say nothing, 'cause they couldn't swear it was me. But they give me eyes like daggers. Oh it was a wicked thing to do. Lord forgive me for that. But I was so young and I thought that was hilarious. I was a bit of a fly-away.

[97] the cutting tables

One time I went to work in a summer dress in the middle of winter. It wasn't because I didn't have anything warm, 'cause I did. But a lady gave me this dress, and I loved it. She was a plumpish lady, but it fitted me. It was a sleeveless white dress, with all pretty white flowers round the top, and I couldn't wait for the summer. It was snowing that day, but I went into the factory wearing it. And they all went: 'Oooh!' 'That's my new dress,' I say. 'Someone give it me.' When I went upstairs to get the socks from the clickers, they all started shivering. Looking back, I can see that Mother had begun to get a bit forgetful by then. She can't have been so observant as she used to be, or she wouldn't have let me go out like that in the cold. I was in the factory about an hour before the forewoman saw me. 'You can't be about here like that. You'll have to go home,' she say. So I went and changed into my warm clothes and went back.

After a few months, I went 'on the board'. That's what they used to call it when you cleaned the shoes. They were finished when they came to the cleaning room, but they were dirty. All sorts of marks on. And you had to make them look good. You couldn't just wipe them over. You had to clean round the line where the sole and the upper joined, the feather-line, as we called it. We did it with our finger nails. We cleaned the patent shoes with petrol. And they come up beautiful. You had the petrol in a little metal container with a round top and a pipe thing what went down into it. You put your duster on the pipe, but sometimes you didn't get enough petrol on it, and that got on your nerves. So you'd lift the lid off, so the petrol was in the open. That was silly really, 'cause you had a torch with a flame coming out at the side of you. That was what you had to run over the shoes after you'd cleaned them. Not to burn them, but to iron the rucks and wrinkles out. What would have happened if we'd had a fire? I never thought about it then, but that make me dodder now. Really, the people in charge should have keep coming round to look what we were doing.

One time, the boss give me and my friend, Violet, some slippers to dress. Black slippers with pink linings. The dressing was a bit sticky, so you had to be pretty experienced. If you did it smudgy, that wouldn't do at all. But when you did it right, the shoes were finished off proper, and they really shone. You had your sponge and your jar of liquid dressing, and you had to hurry, 'cause you had to do a dozen pairs at a time. Violet was doing hers. I was doing mine, getting the dressing on even. Things were going lovely. We were good friends and we talked away to each other while we worked. So that was why I didn't notice the dressing dripping on my hand what was holding the shoe. I was on the last shoe, when I saw that all the pink linings were black. I looked at my hand. It was saturated with black dressing. I was terrified. Violet ran to get Miss Howlett. And I thought: 'Oh no. I'm going to get the sack for this.'

Miss Howlett was a big-featured lady with auburn hair. 'What's happened here?' she said. I was frightened out of my life. I wanted to run home. 'I can't trust you at all. Whatever I give you, you can't do properly,' she said. She put the slippers on a rack and gave me another job. Patent work. I thought when Friday come, she'll give me a week's notice. I lay awake in bed at night. I felt sick, 'cause I really needed the job. Every day, I saw the slippers with black linings what should have been pink. That rack haunted me. Then one morning I see Ethel French take the rack to where she was working. Nice person. She was married to a Canary footballer. I dursen't look too much, but when I looked up again, I saw she was making some paint up. That was pinky paint. She was on the job for two or three days. In them days, they didn't throw nothing away. In the finish, the rack was pushed away. I thought, oh thank you Lord. At least the shoes don't have to be re-cut. When Friday evening come, Miss Howlett come round with a box with all the wages in. She got to us. I thought, oh here it come. She gave Violet her packet first. My little old heart was pounding. Then she give me my wages, and walked off. And I knew I was safe. I really deserved to get the sack, 'cause I should have known better. But when you're fourteen your tongue run away with you, don't it? Of course, I didn't get away with it completely. I was punished for a week, thinking I was going to get the sack. After that you can be sure that my mind was on what I was doing. But I wasn't allowed to do any dressing for ages after that.

⋰∄⋱

I must have been at Batson and Webster's about ten months. And then one day I thought, I won't work here no more. I'll try and get a job at the brewery.[98] So, I went for an interview. Can't remember the man's name, but he said: 'You can start next week. And you are allowed one drink a day.' 'I'll have lemonade,' I say. When I started work, I got a big old khaki overall, like a coat, with a leather apron on

---

[98] Brewing had long been an important Norwich industry. Conditions were ideal, with good local water and abundant supplies of excellent malting barley from the surrounding countryside. As early as 1801, Norwich breweries not only supplied local needs but served markets in London and elsewhere in the country. The industry grew throughout the nineteenth century and the smaller breweries consolidated their production. In the 1920s, when Ethel started work, four companies dominated the market: Bullard's, Morgan's, Steward and Patteson's, and Youngs, Crawshay & Youngs'. When Ethel worked there, production at Steward and Patteson's, the largest brewer of them all, was close to the highest in England. Norwich gained a reputation for the number of its public houses; at the turn of the twentieth century, there were over 500. In Ethel's time it was said that Norwich had a church for every week of the year and a public house for every day.

top. And clogs, wooden clogs with metal toecaps. You had to wear them, because if you dropped a bottle on your toes, you'd break them. We must have looked awful. But I thought that was lovely. Some days, I even went home from work in my clogs and leather apron. I don't know what made me do that.

My friend, Maudie, lost a button from her overall one time. She didn't have a spare one, so she stuck this needle in. She had it a long while, but suddenly one day, while she was working, it went in her leg. When she told me, I said: 'What! Why didn't you use a pin?' A pin wouldn't go through, like a needle do. She had to go up the hospital. They cut her, but every time they go to get the needle out, it moved. She had about five different cuts on her leg, before they got it out. That's why I always say: 'Don't leave no needles about', 'cause they can go in you.

When I first went to the brewery, my job was bottling the light ales and stout. Well, I suppose the machine did it really. One girl put the empties in. There were these big copper vats, ever so huge, and they had taps on that filled the bottles. When the bottle come back round, it was full, so you had to hurry to take it off. If you didn't, it would go round again and overflow. I had to put the cork on top of the bottle and shove it up another machine with my right hand. It went *rrrrr* and tightened the cork. (You couldn't have the beer without being sealed.) Then with my left hand, I put the corked bottles in the case beside me. It was hard work, 'cause they were all pint bottles. There was twenty-four bottles in them crates and I had to shove 'em up on these rollers. I put my weight behind the crate and ran along side it for a little while to get it going. I used to love it.

It was quite a dangerous job really. I was alright, apart from the time a bottle broke when I was pushing it up to tighten the cork. It could easy happen. A bit of glass went in my thumb. The scar's still there. There was one lady told me how she got her hand caught in the machine one time. That could happen if you weren't quick enough. The mechanic happened to be near at the time. He jumped up and switched the machine off. She'd have lost her whole arm if he hadn't. She must have been alright, 'cause she was the one that told me about it but her hand was all scarred. After I'd been there a bit, I thought, oh if only I could do the labelling. That was another machine. You put the bottle in, and held the neck and then a thing came down and put a lovely label on, 'Steward and Patteson's Light Ale' or 'Steward and Patteson's Stout'. I really wanted to do that job, but I never got the chance.

※

After about 15 months at the brewery, I got a bit fed up with the clogs and the leather apron, so I went to Caley's. Someone told me it was lovely working there, 'cause you could eat a lot of chocolate. Whipped cream walnuts, little chocolate whirls, they did do some lovely things.

Girls doing the 'piping' at Caley's factory

I used to make these little whirls with a nut inside. I'd put about ten blobs of chocolate out and a walnut on top. Then I got my bag, with one of these nozzles on the end. You know, like the icing bags you have when you ice a cake. I'd go round, making them lovely little chocolate whirls round the nuts. From time to time, the little hole got blocked. So I had to take the nozzle off and run it through the tap. But for a lot of the girls, that was too much trouble. They just used to suck the stuff out. And of course, it was all germs. And another thing. Sometimes a chocolate would fall on the floor, and it would just be picked up and put back. I ate a lot of chocolate for the first two weeks. But after that, my stomach didn't want any. Especially when I saw some of the things what was done.

At five o'clock in the evening, you had to get a pail of water, scrub all your machine down, and scrub where you worked. One night I was in a hurry, as usual. I fell down with the pail and the water went all over. So I had to clean it up and get another pail of water. I was soaking wet. But I never got the sack like some poor girls, so I must have done something alright.

⌐◃▷⌐

After about six months, I got fed up with Caley's. Where do I go now, I thought. So I went back to the boot work and never looked back. I went to Howlett and White's.[99] Seven shillings a week it was. That was in the machine room. First of all I was doing the backs of the shoe. They're a bit rough where they're joined together and so you put them

---

[99] The Howlett and White factory in Colegate had been the largest shoe factory in the country when it was opened in 1868. It later became Norvic Shoes and continued production until 1973. In the 1980s the site was redeveloped as part of the renovation of the Colegate area.

through a machine what makes the backs go flat. Otherwise, people would have bad heels. When I come off that I went in linings, making the linings that fit in the shoe. I was happy there.

The interior of Howlett and White's factory in Colegate, Norwich c.1913

14. Out on the Town

Maudie and me used to like going to the Easter fair. At that time, the girls were wearing fancy coloured garters. And I had these lovely royal blue ones. They were covered in sequins, and all glittery when the lights used to shine on them. I wouldn't have had the money to buy them if I hadn't been working. The garters were above my knees, but when I went on the roundabout, I made sure that my knees were showing. I only had the one ride, but someone must have seen me. I don't think it were my sisters, 'cause they were all out courting, weren't they? You can bet it was one of the girls what went home and told her mother. And then her mother told my mother. So, the next day, Mother said: 'I want to talk to you.' 'What have I done, Mother?' I say. 'I hear you was showing your legs off on the roundabout. Now don't let me know you do that again.' 'But Mother, I weren't doing nothing.' 'I don't care. You don't do that any more.' You were so innocent in them days. I couldn't believe someone was going to make something out of just a pair of garters on my leg. I suppose some knew about sex, but I didn't. Didn't know nothing about it. And I never knew who told Mother.

Fourteen I was when I had my first high heels. They had a bar over the top, and they were a sort of champagne colour. I wore them with champagne-coloured silk stockings.[100] They had a seam down the

[100] Affordable silk stockings only became available in the 1920s as machines became available for knitting fine silk yarn. Before then, the only stockings available to people with Ethel's means would have been factory-produced, coarse-gauge wool or cotton stockings, generally only available in black or white.

back and a lovely black heelpiece, all zig-zagged. They were about sixpence a pair. You had to be careful when you put them on, and make sure that you had the seam right in the middle, 'cause otherwise you'd get one going north and the other going south. We were smart little girls really. I didn't have a lot of clothes, but I had a little bit more money by then, 'cause I was working. I had one nice skirt and a couple of blouses, so I could wash one out. One time I bought this coat off Maudie's sister, Nelly. It was a lovely green with a beautiful fur collar. And I saved up to buy a camisole[101] with lace straps and satin cami-knickers,[102] and a corset. I never, ever went without a corset. I had a beautiful figure, and I wanted to keep it that way. It was pink. Very pretty and it come all the way down to my bum. The corsets we wore then were them what laced up in the back. You pulled them tight, so you couldn't hardly breathe. They really made you stiff, and they hurt your hip. Most waists were eighteen inches in them days. You didn't see many fat persons.

Maudie and me used to go up the city Tuesdays and Thursdays. There wasn't really anywhere else to go if you didn't have a young man what was in work. And they were few and far between. We'd save up for a pair of 8/11d shoes what we'd wear up the town. But when we felt really well off, we'd get the ones at 10/6d. And they were elite. We only ever wore them on Sundays. I remember the time I got these beautiful, black suede high heels. They had a silver grey snake going round the back and the sides. Really lovely smart shoes. We bought

---

[101] Underwear for the top half of the body, with thin straps that go over the shoulders.

[102] A camisole attached to a pair of knickers.

Ethel (right), her sister Nelly (centre) and a friend

them from a shop that sold rejects cheaply in the Back of the Inns[103] in the city.

Maud and I used to try and dress alike. She didn't copy my shoes, but she always wanted to copy my dress. One time, we each bought a pink raincoat with all little white spots over. But up the city, black and white was the fashion. We had this lady, Mrs Godfrey, what used to make us dresses. She made us both a black silk one with a big, white silk collar. They were longish, and the skirt flared out. Everyone wore a hat in them days. Even after I was married, I always wore a hat. Maudie and me went to Price's one time, and we each bought a big-brimmed felt hat. We cut the rim off, so it was like a helmet. And then we bought two white feathers as big as your hands, and put them one on each side. They were terrible really, but we thought we were the cat's whiskers. One Saturday, I went out on my own. I'll have something different, I thought. So I went into Butcher's, and I bought this lovely hat. It was plum-coloured and on the front there was a corded band of ribbon with all little diamantes on. I think that was

---

[103] Back of the Inns is the name of a street in the Norwich city centre.

about 1/11d. I wore it Sunday. The following week, Maudie bought one.

I didn't do much as regards to hair, but I did have one or two styles, parted in the middle and a Piccadilly. Or sometimes I had a bit of wire over the top of my head with blonde bits on the end. They were like earphones, but you wouldn't see no wire, 'cause I wore an ordinary round hat over it. Just two lovely blonde kiss curls. One on each side. I was dark, but I used to tuck my own hair in, so I looked like I were blonde.

I liked my hair nice for Saturday night, so I used to get it done before I went to work on a Saturday morning. I had to go about half past six, cause I started work at eight o'clock. You paid a shilling for a Marcel.[104] That was when they gave you waves all over with a curling iron. The hairdresser was a bit of a spivvy bloke, [105] but he used to do it good, which is why we all went. He was married, but I heard he'd had to marry her. I went there one morning and he was late. That really messed me about, but rather than leave, I sat there and waited until he turned up. I lost a morning's work and a shilling in wages.

They come out with perms when I was about 16.[106] We liked them 'cause you could just wash your hair and comb it out. You used to

[104] A 'Marcel' is a hairstyle created in the early 1870s by the French hairdresser Marcel Grateau (1852-1936). The Marcel wave imitated the natural curl of the hair. The hairdresser would use hot tongs to produce a curl rather than a crimp. It revolutionized the art of hairdressing and remained popular through into the 1920s.

[105] A 'spiv' is a man, usually dressed in a way that attracts attention, who makes money by dishonest or at least dubious means. During the period of rationing in the 1940s those trading in blackmarket goods were often known as spivs.

[106] The techniques for giving 'permanent' waves to hair had been introduced around the turn of the century. It took several years though before they became widely available in hairdressers catering for a poorer clientèle.

have to pay a guinea, which was a lot of money, so someone would say: 'Let's get up a draw'. The one what ran it had to make sure there was twenty-one people in the draw. You'd all pay a shilling a week for twenty-two weeks, so she earned herself a guinea. We all picked a number out of the hat. So the one what got the first week had it when she'd only paid a shilling. But if you were the last one, you were annoyed, cause it meant you paid for the perm before you had it.

It took hours for a perm. They had to take the bulb out of the light, and plug this round thing in. It was like a crown really, only bigger, with all these sockets hanging down on wires. I don't know why it didn't pull the fitting down. Then they'd roll your hair up on a curler, and stuff it up one of the sockets. It was so heavy when you were all wired up. And you couldn't put your head forward or backward. You'd sit as quiet as anything, but your head would wobble about, and you'd think your neck was going to break at any minute. I was terrified the first time. Talk about going to have a perm, it was more like going to have your head off. So, you had these wires on your head. All sizzling. Smelt terrible. 'Oooh, that's burning,' you'd say. And then they'd come and adjust it. But a lot of people used to end up with burnt heads, cause there was no control. I really think they were dangerous. It's a wonder there weren't people electrocuted. We were so vain, but after we'd had a perm, we didn't feel we wanted it straight again.

I used to stand on the fender in front of the living room mirror to put my lipstick on. That was naughty and my poor old father used to shout: 'Get off of that fender. You'll get set alight!' Horrible old man, I thought. Of course, over the years, I came to realise that I could easily have got set alight. And once you got the flames on the frocks like we used to have, there was no way of putting them out. We wouldn't stand no chance. I put lipstick and powder on, but if Father see me with too much, I'd have to take it off. So I'd put more on when I got out of the house. In the finish I got so I always went in the toilet down the bottom of the yard to get made up. I sat on the lav seat, with my cosmetics on my lap and I done it. At that time of day, if you had a beauty spot, you were beautiful. We used to think that the scales what come off the winkles looked like beauty spots. So, we stuck 'em on our face. I can't remember using any sticky stuff. We just spit on them. We didn't have the art of making up or anything. So I expect we looked like a lot of clowns when we did.

Maudie and I used to go dancing on a Monday evening. We'd go home from work to get washed and tidied up, and get some decent things on. We didn't have a lot to wear, but what we had, we made good use of. One night we'd put a bow or ribbon on our blouse. Then another time, we'd make it into a tie. If we didn't have more than one blouse, we used to wash it out, and iron it. And they were terrible irons. We made our hair look nice. And we had nice shoes when we

The Bandstand and Pavilion in Chapelfield Gardens

went to places like that. Powdering up, putting lipstick on – we were grown-ups now.

Maudie would come and knock at my door, and I'd be ready. Sometimes we'd go to a dance in Earlham Park. That was quite a long way and we had to walk all the way. I don't think the buses ran there, and anyway, we couldn't afford the bus fare. We had more money on Mondays than we had for the rest of the week, but we still had to scrape up the sixpence to get into that dance. They were more expensive than the ones at Chapelfield Gardens[107] because they were proper dances with big bands. One time I only had five pennies and three farthings. This boy, Billy was walking in with me. He was a nice young man, but of course, he didn't have no money to give me. And I thought how am I going to get in? The man was at the gate and as I went in, I just threw the money in his hand and ran. I don't know what I'd have done if he'd have called me back. Billy were a good-looking boy, and we had a lovely evening. 'Could I take you home?' he said. When we got the top of the lokes[108] where the brewery is, we were standing talking when the dog come running round and sniffing. Father didn't see us, but the dog did. Flossy, its name was. Father shouted: 'Ethel, where are you? Come in.' I felt so embarrassed. You

[107] Chapelfield Gardens was opened as a public park in the heart of the Norwich City Centre in 1880 during the childhood of Ethel's parents. The land originally belonged to the Chapel of St Mary and had been tucked inside the mediaeval city walls. During the 14th century, it had been the site for compulsory archery practice. In 1792, the site had turned into a reservoir to meet the growing city's need for water. In the colder winters in the early 19th century, it was used as an ice-skating rink. It was restored back to open ground in 1853 but was left wild and untended. There were complaints in the 1860s and 70s that it was being used as a meeting place for 'undesirables'. This pushed the authorities into cleaning it up and converting it to a public park complete with a two-storey Grand Pavilion, a bandstand, gardens and play area.

[108] Small roads.

really feel things when you're young. And the boy? I thought what am I going to do when I see him again? How am I going to face him? My father was a menace. I thought he was a beast for coming after me.

Most Monday evenings, we went to a dance in Chapelfield Gardens. There was crowds going in, the same boys as were up Prince of Wales Road, so we knew a lot of them. And apart from us young'uns of fourteen onwards, there was them that were more matured, seventeen and eighteen-year-old boys and girls. That was tuppence to get in. The men in the band had white pants, and red tops with a little bit of gold on. Clean looking young men. They always looked smart, with their brylcreemed[109] hair, all plastered back. The bandleader used to come and say a few words before the dancing. And then they'd play all the old tunes what was wonderful. There was concrete all the way round the bandstand, so you weren't dancing on dirt. If no one came up and asked you to dance, you were a wallflower for the evening, 'cause at that time of day, you didn't dance with a young woman. Our ambition was to get in and get a partner and that all depended what girls were there. If they were better than you, the boys would take them. Obviously there was some girls that were a bit flighty, but the boys knew which girls they could respect. If a boy liked you, he'd try and keep with you all night. At the end, we had mostly waltzes, which was lovely. 'Girl of my dreams I love you', 'Drifting and Dreaming', 'Charmaine', and all them lovely old songs. If a boy thought you were his sort, he'd probably ask to walk you home, but we had to be home by ten.

---

[109] Brylcreem was a greasy cream used to slick down combed hair to give it a neat, shiny look. During the Second World War, it was particularly popular with Royal Air Force pilots who became known as the 'Brylcreem Boys'.

Some evenings, Maudie and me would go up the city. We'd walk through Barrack Street, and over the bridge past Tombland and then we'd turn left at Prince of Wales Road. We'd always go down on the left hand side, what we called the 'sixpenny side'. Then we'd cross over at Thorpe Station and go back on the other side. That was the 'half-crown side'. I don't know why they said that. But we thought there was a better class of people went on that side. My sister, Nelly went up the city in the week, but she'd never put her best coat on, 'cause she was saving it for Sundays. She was very tight on money. So one night I thought, I'd borrow this coat. But I didn't know she was up the city herself. Anyway, there was her on the 'sixpenny side' and me on the 'half crown side' with her best coat and fur collar. She was furious. She wouldn't show me up outside, but she was waiting for me when I got home. She pulled the coat off me and she didn't half give me a clout on the head. Well, I wasn't going to have her hitting me, so I hit her back. Poor Nelly. I was more robust than her. But I dursen't take her things any more.

Time went quick when you were out. You'd stop and speak to the boys, and show off. You know, like kids do. If a boy liked you, he'd say: 'What time you going home?' He'd have to ask you straight away, 'cause you weren't allowed to stand around too long. If you were in a doorway, a policeman would come and move you out. Oh yes, there was policemen on each side of the road. We knew all their names. There was one what had a baby face. And the boys used to say: 'Look, here come Babyface.' He was the one what used to kick them in the ankles.

Whatever time you said you were leaving, the boy would be waiting for you. He'd just walk with you. Wouldn't hold your arm nor nothing. I didn't have many boys take me home, and I couldn't understand why. I used to think, I'm as good-looking as her and she's always getting someone. I had this boy once, Jack, his name was, and I remember going on Mousehold with him and sitting on a form. He didn't kiss me nor nothing. But I can remember him singing to me 'I can't give you anything but love, baby'. Of course, that didn't mean nothing. He took me to the pictures. We went in the 1/3d.s, but then I didn't see him no more. And then there was another one what took me home, but I didn't let him take me to the pictures. He sung to me an' all: 'The moon was all aglow, and heaven was in your eyes, the night that I told you, those little white lies'. I suppose they must have liked me, but they didn't kiss me nor nothing.

⚜

'It's Skivvies' night tonight.'[110] That's what we used to say when we were up the city on a Wednesday night. These were the girls what come from the country to work in the big, posh houses on Unthank Road. In them days they were rich people what lived in them, and they all wanted servants. We didn't know a lot ourselves, but these poor little girls didn't see or hear anything in the country. And they couldn't get jobs there. They were from a different culture. You could tell straight away that they weren't from Norwich. Rosy cheeks and round faces. Nice healthy girls, although I don't know how long they kept their rosiness, shut up in them houses. They dressed different to us.

---

[110] During Ethel's childhood, domestic service was the largest single source of employment for women. Almost all of the young people in service were country born and bred. Country girls were preferred because they were generally healthier, harder working and more deferential and honest than girls brought up in the towns. In addition, most town girls knew of the long hours, hard work, and low pay that domestic service involved and preferred to work in factories, where they could earn more and enjoy more freedom.

They weren't modern. Most of them used to wear black dresses and black coats, long and a little bit drab. And they all wore them pull-on-hats what go all round. They didn't have no brims.

The girls lived up the top in the attics. Some of them stayed there for years, 'cause that was regular money, and they got their keep. Poor things. The mistress of the home wouldn't be doing any manual work, so you can bet she piled it on 'em. And you can bet she didn't care two hoots what she were giving them to do. Up at five in the morning, cleaning the great old grates out, black-leading 'em, getting coal in, getting wood in, getting the breakfast ready, and scrubbing the linen. And then they had to clean the ovens out. They were them big black old ovens. That was a hard life, and no doubt they had to give their mother most of their wages. They were working all weekend. It was only Wednesday evening they had off.

I can remember Charlie saying that one of his pals once went back to the house with one of the maids. Probably the family was on holiday. I don't think they done nothing wrong, but they had a whale of a time. Cups of tea and cocoa. Mostly though, we didn't have much contact with them. I can't ever remember standing and talking to them. We were naughty calling them skivvies. We thought we were better than them but that was wrong. We were just fortunate to be in the cities, so we didn't have to leave our parents.

15. Struggling to Cope

One day my world was shattered. I was fourteen years old. I come home from work for dinner and when I got in the living room, the broom was up in the corner and the mats were up outside. That wasn't like Mother, and I knew she wouldn't be out at dinnertime. I shouted: 'Mother, where are you?' There was no answer, so I ran upstairs. And there she was. Laid on the bed with all her clothes on. I yelled: 'Mother, Mother, what's the matter?' She looked at me and said: 'Where's your mother gone? Where's your mother gone?' I couldn't believe it. My own mother couldn't recognize me. I was terrified. I couldn't think straight. I ran up the road for my sisters, 'cause they all lived near. They sent for the doctor, and he said she'd had a stroke. He didn't do nothing. He only come the once, 'cause they didn't do anything for strokes in them days. But from then on, poor Mother was like a child. She couldn't get her teeth in. She couldn't do anything for herself. Everything was painful for her. She didn't know anything or anybody really. She got fat, bless her. She had to have her wedding ring on her little finger. I felt like it was the end of my world.

Nelly was a machinist, but she had to give up her job to look after Mother. Not that Mother were ever any trouble, but of course, she couldn't be left alone. Poor Nelly. If you were at home in them days, you were at everyone's beck and call. You were a lackey. I think Father give her a shilling a week, but that wasn't much for a girl of eighteen. She was a puny little girl, but she looked after Mother really well. She washed her all over every week, and put her clean clothes on. Mother only had one decent skirt, and now she didn't have to do no work we put her in that one all the time. She always had a nice blouse, and I used to comb her lovely black hair. But sometimes she'd cry: 'I haven't been washed. Look at my linen. I haven't had clean things on for months.' Some days, I'd be black-leading the old stove. I'd be sweating, and all of a sudden I'd look up. I'd see two lily-white feet in a nightdress, and Mother would be standing there. Oh, that used to make me jump. I'd say: 'Mother, you get back to bed, love. You can't get up for a little while.'

Poor Mother. I think her mind had got so het up with all the washing and cleaning and shopping and making ends meet, that it wouldn't never rest. She always liked a couple of shillings in her purse (probably had more money than what we did), but one day she couldn't find it. She started crying: 'I've lost my purse.' We looked under the pillows. We pulled the mattress up, but we couldn't find this purse. And all the time Mother was crying: 'I lost my money. I lost my money.' In the end, we found it behind a picture in the living room. Another time she got it into her head that she wanted something from the shop. But she couldn't tell us what it was. I went to Mrs Howlett's and I said: 'Oh, Mrs Howlett, please can I bring my mother over, and can you tell her that you haven't got whatever she wants. She's really upset. She keep crying and we don't know what to do with her.' And Mrs Howlett say: 'All right, my dear, you bring her in.' I went and got Mother. I held her arm and opened the shop door. I say: 'Mother want something, Mrs Howlett. 'Ooh,' she say: 'I'm right out of them. They'll be coming in soon and I'll let you know.' Mother was then satisfied.

After Mother's stroke, my sister Edie used to come down to ours on a Monday. She was a hardworking woman. She used to bring her washing and she'd do ours an' all. That's when she saw that Nelly was getting a bit down. So after a few months, she say: 'I should think poor little Nelly want to go back to work. Arthur don't come home to dinner, and so I can come every day if you like.' After that, Edie came over every day on her bike. Of course, she had to leave as soon as Nelly got home, cause she lived a good way, and she had to be back in time for Arthur's tea. She didn't charge nothing, so Nelly got her money again.

The rest of the family didn't come after Mother got ill. She didn't even know. Edie and Nelly and me looked after her from morning till night, while Father just went his own little way. But Saturday nights, he was supposed to come home from the pub early, so I could go to the pictures with Maudie. Most weeks I'd be sitting in doors, biting my nails, wondering where he were. When is Father coming? We always had to book seats ahead, 'cause I was never sure what time he would be home. Sometimes I'd have to go and hunt him up. If I hadn't have went after him, he wouldn't have come back. I used to worry about Maudie. It weren't her responsibility, but she had to bear the brunt as well. She had to sit with Mother while I ran to try and find Father. And I never knew where he was. There was pubs all along Barrack Street, and he went in all of 'em. I'd go in two or three, and when I found him, I'd say: 'Come on Father, I'm now going to the pictures. Maudie and me got tickets.' He'd come, but he didn't like it and he used to be grumpy. It weren't fair. It was his wife and he should have been taking care of her. Sometimes we had to miss the beginning of the picture.

I don't know what happened while we were at the pictures. I don't know if he treated her right when we weren't there. After her stroke, they had their bed downstairs, and once when I was in the living room, I heard her making funny noises. 'What you doing to her?' I shouted. 'What's happening? Why's she making them noises?' I was a bit naughty to do that I suppose, but I was worried. And he didn't like it. He come through into the living room. 'Don't you dictate to me,' he said. 'Well I am,' I say. You see she couldn't say nothing. She couldn't tell me why she was crying. I don't know for sure what he was doing to her, but something did come into my mind. You see he weren't that old, and I suppose he might have tried to do something to her. And that's why I shouted. She was like a baby, and she wouldn't have understood anything like that. Poor old love.

The rest of us did our best for Mother. My older sisters what were married, they were good girls. They didn't have a lot of money, but they took her to Yarmouth one time. That must have been nice, sitting in her little deck chair and going in an open landau. Nelly and I bought her a chair. It was the first time she had a chair of her own. We got it

Mother at Yarmouth

for sixpence a week. 'Mother, that's your chair,' we said. It had just ordinary wood arms, but the seat was lovely velvet, and all padded at the back. We helped her in, but it was hard. We weren't very big and she was a big woman. When we lifted her up she cried out because of

**Hilda, Mother, Hilda's daughter Irene, Clara, Edie and Rose
with Hilda's son in front, all in the landau**

this arm. And I used to say: 'Oh Nelly, I wish we could have got that other cushion.' That would have made it higher for her. When you think about it, that would have only been an extra three ha'pence a week. But she got a lot of happiness out of that chair, she really did.

≍⊨

People got depressed in them days, just like today, but the doctors then didn't know how to handle them. They just sent them up to the asylum,[111] separated from other people, and no doubt, they got worse and worse. That was terrible really. I never seen the asylum, but I heard about it, 'cause Fred's first wife, Sarah, ended up in there. Poor

[111] During the period to which Ethel is referring, lunatic asylums, (including the one in Thorpe just outside the city boundary that served the inhabitants of Norwich), housed together people suffering from all forms of mental difficulty: those with arrested mental development, often congenital in nature, then called 'idiots' and 'imbeciles'; those with disorders on the autistic spectrum; those with psychotic diseases such as schizophrenia; those suffering from depression; and those mentioned by Ethel who might simply have been overwhelmed by the stress of their living situations. There were few effective treatments and those who were discharged probably benefited most from a remission brought on by the passage of time.

Sarah. She was a gaunt-looking lady. I never see her with any teeth in. And she was as old as my mother. I think Albert had something to do with her at one time. He and Fred were both nice-looking blokes, and I don't know how they got involved. I can remember someone telling me that they tossed for who was going to marry her. And that's the truth. She was a widow and she already had a son and a daughter. So Fred married her and took on these two children. And then he had a daughter with her, my niece, little Edie. She was about my age. Well, Sarah went a bit funny in the head. One time when Fred was away, she went down to the riverside and tried to drown herself. Somebody saved her, but Fred couldn't take care of her, so he had to put her in the asylum. It's sad when your brain go and you lose your mind. Little Edie then had to go and live with her stepsister what lived in a two-roomed house up Coberg Street. They were all slums round there. The sister had quite a family of her own, but with Sarah going in the asylum and Fred working away a lot, there was no one else to look after Edie.

My friend, N's mother had to go in the asylum. She was a beautiful lady, but unfortunately, she had this little baby on the change, and she got this post-natal thing come on her. Women today can get it after they've had a baby, but now they give you drugs, which get you on your feet again. In my day, no one recognized it, so, of course, there was no treatment. She wasn't very old, but she got so she couldn't converse with you, and she couldn't look after the children. After a few weeks they took her away. And I never heard no more about her. I suppose there were a lot like her about.

One day, after her mother had gone, I said to N: 'If you come and keep my mother company, I'll come and clean your windows.' I started with the ones upstairs. They were sash windows and to clean the outsides, you had to sit out on the windowsill. You then had to pull the top window down and press it down hard on your knees. Very tricky. You were up quite high, and there was nothing to lean on. Never thought nothing of it at the time, but if I'd had one false move, I'd have been out backwards, and I'd probably have broken my back. So, there I was, high up on their windowsill, cleaning the windows. Then, just as I was getting to the last big window, my heart missed a beat. A man was peeping round the door at me. It was N's father. But he didn't come in like any ordinary man would and say hello. My heart was pounding. I've got to get out of here, I thought. I squiggled back inside, 'cause I didn't want to fall backwards and kill myself. Then I shut the window and I went down to the kitchen. The man weren't there, so I thought I'll just clean the window. I weren't tall enough to clean it on a step or a stool, so I sat out on the sill with my knees over the sink. And then, all of a sudden, this man was there again. If he'd only said: 'Hello love how are you? Are you helping?' But he didn't say anything. He just come in and touched my knee and I had this horrible sensation go through me. He didn't do anything more. He didn't get chance to, but if I'd been a little girl what'd let him, you can bet that he would have.[112] I shut the window up and I ran home. 'Your father's looking for you,' I say to N. I felt right sick. It lasted days with me and I never went back no more. I suppose he was all right with his own children. But I bet that sort of thing did happen, and the little

---

[112] Hard figures are impossible to compile but incidences of abuse of children and young women were not at all uncommon in this period. Only the most egregious cases were ever reported to the police. Many who would today be imprisoned as paedophiles lived untroubled in their communities.

kids were too frightened to say anything. I never told no one about it. I never said nothing to N. 'cause I didn't want her to feel bad. I couldn't tell my mother, 'cause she was senile. I dursen't tell my father. It was a very, very frightening episode in my life. And I haven't said anything about it till now.

⊰⊱

In my day, most people made room for their parents when they got old or sick. Nearly every family had an elderly mother and father come and live with them at some time. It didn't matter if they had ten kids. People generally did rally round to help each other, 'cause the pension was only ten shillings a week and the old people couldn't live on that. So why did Uncle Billy die in the workhouse?[113] I never understood He'd had all that money and yet he finished his days in that terrible place. We knew he wasn't a good man, but why did he have to end up there? Why didn't his children take care of him?[114]

[113] The Norwich workhouse was situated on Bowthorpe Road on the site that later became the West Norwich Hospital. It was built soon after the 1834 Poor Law Reform Act which provided that the able-bodied poor should no longer be given relief payments out of local authority funds but, instead, be accommodated in workhouses that were so awful that only the desperate would apply for admission. In a typical Victorian workhouse the daytime hours were spent on hard labour, such as stone-breaking or picking apart old ropes (oakum); the food was minimal and unattractive; and the night was spent with minimal blankets in large unheated dormitories. By Ethel's time, the workhouse had become less intimidating and housed mainly sick and elderly. An observer in 1910 described how the Norwich Workhouse management tried to house the 'respectable old' separately so that they did not need 'to associate with the kind of people whom he or she has never associated with before.' Despite this, he said: 'the indescribable workhouse atmosphere is just as all-pervading in Norwich as elsewhere. Any attempt to deal with all classes of people, old and young, good and bad, sane and insane, under the same roof is inevitably doomed to failure.' Two articles in the *Norwich Mercury* in November 1920 are illuminating. One reported the debate about whether a pint of beer should be provided to the residents on Christmas Day and another reported the death of a 57 year-old man who had cut his throat after saying that 'rather than go into the infirmary, I will do myself in.'

[114] Uncle Billy was presumably in the infirmary wing of the workhouse. He would have been admitted there because of his blindness and dementia.

When Nelly and me heard that he was in the workhouse we said: 'We'll call in and see him.' We didn't bear no grudge, 'cause he didn't treat Mother right. We weren't like that. We went in and we asked about Billy Chaplin. A man took us to this room, and there he was, sitting on a huge mattress in a big square cot. It was like a playpen for a child, but in a big form. That had rods all the way round, so he couldn't get out or in. That was gruesome. He were a big man, and blind then. I don't know if he knew us, but we went in and said hello. Of course, Mother had wished a lot of bad things on him, 'cause he was so wicked. But I don't think she really meant it. I thought if she could see him now, she'd be sorry.

It was a sad thing for anyone to end up in the workhouse. I remember going to my brother Graham's one Sunday. Him and his wife Ethel lived with her mother and father, 'cause they had three bedrooms. And this Sunday, Ethel, was crying. She was ever so upset. 'Why you crying, Ethel?' I say. And she said: 'Uncle Tom's gone in the workhouse.' He wasn't really her uncle, but he'd lived with them for years and years, and so he was like family. He used to work for the corporation. I don't know if he were on the dustbins or what, but he had a good job. I suppose he earned about twenty-five shillings a week, and you can bet he was giving them a pound. And then for them to let him go in the workhouse. I can't understand why he had to go when he retired. He'd have got ten shillings a week pension. Why couldn't they have took half? Or even eight or nine shillings?

16. Finding Dick and Losing Mother

It was about this time that I started seeing this boy, Dick when I was up the city. Very dark. Beautiful white teeth. I remember walking behind him on Prince of Wales Road and thinking how lovely looking he was. I was fascinated by him. I couldn't stop looking at him. But at the same time, I didn't want nothing to do with him, 'cause he seemed smutty. I don't mean I ever heard him say really bad things. Just dirty jokes. I think he just wanted to show off. But still I was shocked, 'cause I weren't used to anyone talking like that. I was ever such a prude. I saw him down Yarmouth once. He was with Alfie and some of the other boys that I used to be more friendly with. And he just came up and kissed me. Not on the lips. On the face. But he evidently fancied me. Every time I saw him, he say: 'Can I walk home with you?' And I thought: 'Oh please, Lord, don't let me love him.'

I used to let Alfie take me home sometimes. Just walk me home. Not kiss me or anything. I didn't really want that, and he never asked. Then one morning, a girl who worked at the brewery with me asked: 'How d'you get on last night?' 'All right,' I said. 'Alfie took me home.' 'No,' she say: 'Alfie took *me* home. And I said: 'How could he take you home? He took *me* home.' 'Well he did,' she said. So I said: 'What time?' Well it turned out that he took her home after ten o'clock. And I was already home then. Of course, he was entitled to do what he wanted. There wasn't nothing between us. He'd never even kissed me. But I was really upset. My ego had gone down to the floor. I thought I was the one and only what could have this boy, and that he'd go home satisfied, just talking to me. I suppose he got a cuddle with her.

The next time I saw Alfie, I turned my head away. And then I see Dick. Ah I thought. I know he like me. If he ask me tonight, I'm going to let him take me home and show that other one what I think about him. How indignant you are when you're young. What did it matter that Alfie had walked another girl home after me? So I went up to Dick and I said: 'Do you want to take me home?' Well, he could have said, no, 'cause I'd said no to him so many times. But he said: 'Yes, of course I do.' And then I thought, oh crumbs, he's smutty. I'm going to have trouble with him. Nobody had told me, but I knew in my heart that I shouldn't let no one touch me until I met the right one and got married. I worried all the way going along Riverside Road. But he was ever so well behaved. He put me on the inside of the path. And we walked along just talking. He was lovely. He came as far as the top of the lokes. My house was a little way further up the road, but I didn't dare go there with him. Father used to come out with the dog, and he'd have killed me if he'd seen me with a boy. We stood talking a little while. And then he said to me: 'Can I kiss you?' 'Yes, if you want to, I said.' He's nice, I thought. He's not going to do nothing smutty. He wouldn't have asked to kiss me if he was. So he kissed me, and straight away I thought I love this boy.

I saw him again the next night, but he didn't ask to walk me home. He just said hello. And I thought, oh my goodness, he probably didn't like kissing me. I reckon it was the tea-leaves. I'd had a pickled onion for my tea that night, and I didn't want my mouth to smell of onion when I went up the city. I didn't have the money to buy them little cashews to make my breath smell nice. So I ate some tea-leaves to take the onion smell away. Well, you can bet they smelt worse than the onion. Alfie didn't ask to walk me home no more after I gave him the cold shoulder. And I thought that was that as far as Dick was concerned.

But then the next time I met Dick, he said: 'Can I walk you home?' And of course I said: 'Oh yes.' That was lovely. He walked me home and then he put his arm round me and kissed me. Oh that was romantic. And after that, he kept walking me home from the city. He give me a photo of himself and one day when I was brushing Mother's hair, I shew her. 'Mother, this is my young man, who I'm going to marry,' I say. Of course, he weren't really my young man then. He was only walking me home. We hadn't even had a date. And anyhow, poor Mother couldn't understand what I was saying,

❄

Sometimes our sister Rose helped look after Mother. She was married to a warrant officer in the Air Force and, when he went away, she used to come home and take over the house. She didn't pay no board or anything, and when I got home I still had to wash up and do the ironing. She was a bit bossy, but that did give me and Nelly a break from doing everything. One morning Rose woke me up about six o'clock. 'Ethel, come downstairs quick,' she said. 'See Mother before she go.' But when I got downstairs in my nightclothes, she'd gone. Of course I was upset, but I couldn't take it in at the time. I was only sixteen, and I'd never known anyone die before. I said I wanted to go to work, 'cause I couldn't bear being at home. But I was crying and crying, so they had to send me home.

We kept the coffin in the front room. Some people put a black plank of wood up at the front window when a dead person was there, but I don't think we did. We kept the coffin open, but we had a sheet over it. We put a pail of disinfectant with an onion under it. That way there weren't no smells, cause the onion took them away. Before the funeral, a lot of people come in to look at the corpse. It was a mark of respect. Mother's friends from Cavalry Street come. 'Let's have a look at your mother,' they said. Brother Albert, the eldest, come in every morning before he went to work. He used to go in and lift up the sheet and look at her. I don't know why he done it. I heard that dead bodies could bust open. Whether that's true or not, I don't know, but Mother was a big person and I suppose that could have happened. So Albert took a chance coming in and looking at her every morning. She was in the front room for about a week. Then on the last day, they screwed down the lid. Brother Walter came in and brought a crown of all beautiful, coloured flowers and that just said on: 'For her glory, well done.' We cried when that come. We all knew that Mother had done well, and she deserved her crown.

The girls all had new clothes for the funeral. You definitely didn't go to a funeral without everything black. My sister Rose got it all organized. That must have cost quite a bit, but Mother had always made sure she was insured. A penny a week. You had your father insured for more money than anyone else, 'cause he was the wage-earner, but in them days most people insured so they could be buried right, with dignity. (When kids used to ask their mother: 'Can you buy me this?' there were some what used to say: 'When your nanny die and we get the insurance money you can have something.') Not having enough money for your funeral – oh that would have been most degrading. Of course there were them what didn't have it. They had to be buried in a pauper's grave. I think they just put them in a box and buried them.[115]

At Mother's funeral, it was all dead black. The men in the family had black suits and black ties. I had a black dress, black stockings, black shoes, black hat, and a black coat with a fur collar, 'cause it was cold. At that time, the coats had flare bottoms, and low waists. Just before we left home, brother Walter gave a beautiful prayer. He had a lovely voice, soft and soothing. The funeral procession must have been a sight to see, going through the streets. The hearse was beautiful, all glass, covered in flowers. The cabs were black. Seven of them in all. The horses were black. The funeral men had black suits and tall black silk hats. Everyone stood still when we went past. They bowed their heads and the men took their caps off. After the service was over we went home. The girls put a nice tablecloth on and we had a good spread.

❧

After the funeral I was ever so ill. I used to bust out crying in the street. 'Mother, why did you leave us?' People would say: 'What's the matter with you, dear?' But I couldn't tell them. I'd never had no one die before, and to lose my mother. If that'd been my father, I might not have been so upset. But my mother! For weeks I used to cry out

---

[115] Although incomes were extremely limited, most working people in this period managed to make contributions to a friendly society in order to provide a payout on their demise that would be sufficient to pay for a decent funeral. The subscriptions would be paid weekly to the insurance man who would visit the house. Being forced into the workhouse and being buried in a pauper's grave were the two great fears that haunted the parents of Ethel's generation. It was feared that the dead would not lie peacefully if the funeral were not paid for. Paupers were placed in cheap coffins and often buried with five other similar coffins in a communal grave, unmarked by any headstone. Earlier (p.76) Ethel recounts the extraordinary efforts her mother made to ensure that a baby that had died was buried decently.

in the street. In the end, my sisters took me to the pub for a drink one night. 'Ethel,' they said, 'you're going to have a Guinness.' I said I didn't want one 'cause I didn't drink. But they say: 'You get that down you, 'cause if you don't pull yourself together, you'll go in an asylum.' So I drank this big old glass of Guinness. It was horrible. But they'd frightened the life out of me. I didn't want to go in the asylum. I never drank no more Guinness, but after that, I pulled myself together. For years and years, the family used to go up to Mother's grave every Sunday, the married ones and all. We'd take turns buying flowers, 'cause we didn't have a lot of money.

Nelly got married soon after Mother died, and so I was the lady of the house. I managed the money and everything for my two brothers and Father. We got on our feet a bit then, because for a while we were all working, Charlie, Frank, Father and me. I didn't want to stay at home all day. I thought I'm not going to be a lackey. At first, there was quite a lot of money, so I had the house done out. I spent quite a bit. I had new curtains. I had the living room decorated. But later on Father and my brother Frank lost their jobs and couldn't get no more work. They just got a few shillings from the bureau, but still we done alright. Rich Charlie, he always used to pay his board, and there was my money an' all. Sometimes Charlie say: 'I'm going to bring Maud [his girl friend] to tea tonight.' So, I'd get a tin of crab for eleven pence and a small tin of salmon for about sixpence. I'd make a few buns, and I'd soak some dried fruit and boil it up. We'd have quite a nice tea. I was walking in Mother's steps. I did everything like she did.

※

After Mother died, we had brother Fred's daughter Edie live with us. Edie's mother, Fred's first wife had died in the asylum by then, and

Fred had married again to a lady what had a disfigurement – a great big liver-like thing that covered half her face. It was a shame, 'cause the other half was lovely. She met Fred in the Robin Hood and, knowing he didn't have his wife, she offered to keep his house clean. She was married to an elderly man at the time, and when he found out about Fred, he threw her out. Fred took her in and when the old man died, he married her. She had two children with her. They only had one bedroom, so how they all slept I don't know. Edie had to keep living with her stepsister 'cause there was no room for her. So when I saw her up the city one day, I asked her if she wanted to come and live with us. I don't know why but Father never went back into the front bedroom after Mother died. He moved in with the boys. I moved into the front bedroom. So that left the third bedroom for Edie.

17. Courting Days

One day I come home from work, and when I opened my gate, I saw brother Charlie boxing with Dick. Charlie wasn't usually there at that time of day. He was the one what had a good job. But that day he was off work, 'cause he hadn't been well. Father was home too. He and my brother Frank were mostly out of work in them days. Charlie and Dick weren't close friends, but they were pals. They knew each other from the lads' club[116] up the city. I ran up the steps past them, 'cause I was embarrassed. 'Dick's here, and me in my old truck,'[117] I thought. I washed my face, put a little powder on, and tidied myself up. Then I got the best cups out of the front room, the china cups with the blue and gold. Father didn't like it at all. He was very abrupt. 'What you got them cups out for?' he say. I tell him: 'When we have visitors, Father, we always give them nice cups.' The ones we had every day were just ordinary cups, and odd ones at that. We never had two alike. But the china cups had saucers, and a sugar basin and jug to match.

The next time I went up the city, Dick come up to me and said: 'Can I take you to the pictures?' I said: 'Oh yes.' He took me to the Regent. There was always crowds in the queue for the pictures in them days. So he booked tickets for 1/3d each. That way we knew our seat would still be there, even if we got in a bit late. We sat down. He

---

[116] During the late 19th century, lads' clubs were set up throughout the country by social reformers to keep young men off the streets and to provide them with opportunities to improve their physical fitness and moral character. They were targeted at the poorer elements of the city's population, those most likely to get into trouble. This would still have been true during the 1920s when Dick was attending.

[117] Old clothes

didn't get hold of my hand or nothing. But he did put a box of chocolates on my lap. It was only tiny, but I thought, oh that's lovely. And then, I felt something in my throat. I thought if he hear me cough he won't fancy me. And of course, when you cough, there's phlegm. So all through that picture, I was sitting there with this cough in my throat. I thought, if only I could get rid of it. But I dursen't. I just sat there, stiff and starched. Rigid and not opening his chocolates, wondering whether he'd go with me any more. When the old film was over, we went outside. I hadn't eaten his chocolates. I hadn't spoken to him. And then, as we were walking up the road, I saw a big lorry coming. Now I can cough, I thought. But I didn't time it right, so he heard me anyhow. I might just as well have done it in the pictures. All that agony all night. Seeing a picture what I couldn't enjoy. Didn't hold his hand cause I was so frightened I'd cough and the phlegm would come up. Anyway, he walked me home, and after that we were together.

⊰⧉⊱

Dick was a very hard worker, but he was out of work for a long time. In 1931, nearly all the men were. They earned more money than the women, so I suppose that's why the bosses got rid of as many of them as they could. All I know is that I never got stood off. I was back in the boot work then and for a lot of the year we had loads of work plus overtime. But then there were other times when we might only have five half days. For three months at a time, we might never know what it was to have a full week's money. In that time, it was a lot easier to get work if you knew the foreman. The fathers got their sons in, and the sons got their sons in. That was more or less how it was done. But poor Dick didn't have no-one to get him in. Every day he used to go to the Co-op with his packet of tools. If someone didn't turn up and they were pushed for workers, they could set you on in the middle of the morning. The man there was very nice. He liked Dick and he say: 'Boy, you want a job bad don't you?' But they couldn't keep him. He'd perhaps get two days work and that would be it. And of course, he had to tell them down at the bureau that he were working. So he wouldn't put his cards in for them two days.[118]

Dick wore out most of his things when he was out of work. He had holes in the bottom of his shoes like the palm of your hand. But he still used to come and see me every night. Every night, two miles from his house to mine. He put a bit of cardboard in to cover up the holes. And then another piece for when he was walking back. I remember once, I had his shoes mended for him. Mostly we went for a walk. Sometimes we walked on Mousehold Heath to the mussel ranger's house. We used to sit on this form and hold hands and kiss.

Dick only got about eight shillings bureau money. I used to give him a shilling now and then, and sometimes when he come round, he'd say: 'My grandpa gave me a shilling today, Ethel. We can go to the pictures.' That was two five-penny seats, and a quarter of licorice allsorts when we were there, or a penn'orth of chips when we come out. That was our lot, and then we had to walk all the way home. We went to the Hippodrome one night. They were full up, but this bloke on the door, he say: 'I'll put you in the boxes.' And he did. But honestly, I was embarrassed. I didn't want no one to see us, 'cause of Dick's poor old coat.[119]

---

[118] i.e. would not declare himself as unemployed at the labour bureau.

[119] The boxes were round the sides of the theatre between the stalls and the circle levels and, thus, their occupants were highly visible.

Before he walked home, he used to come in the house and I'd make him a cup of cocoa. Then we'd stand in the yard and kiss goodnight. But one particular night he wouldn't come in. 'I'm not going to keep courting with you,' he said. 'My bureau money's finished and I can't see myself getting a job.' At that time of day, you only got so many weeks bureau money, and that was it. And of course, that was the big depression. He said: 'It's not fair to you. You could get someone else, what's got a good job and where you'd have something to look forward to.' What matters, I thought? I can treat him now and again to the pictures. I ran in crying. My brother Charlie, he say: 'What's the matter with you?' At first, I couldn't tell for crying. My heart was really broken. Charlie, he say: 'Don't cry. Don't worry about it.' But he couldn't do anything about it could he?

Next day I say to my friend, Maudie: 'Dick's not going to get no more bureau money, and he don't want to keep with me no more.' She weren't courting then, and so we went a couple of nights up the city. But then I say: 'I in't going out no more.' I didn't want to speak to these silly boys, and I didn't want to see Dick if he didn't want to continue our friendship. We stayed in for about three weeks, but then one night, I said: 'Shall we go on Mousehold tonight?' It was a lovely place in summer. There was a bandstand and a band playing, and hundreds of people. We walked by some boys what were playing cards in a ring. And there he was. My heart went all funny, but I didn't go near him. No, I thought. He said we aren't courting anymore. He looked up at me, but he didn't say nothing. My heart started to pound, and I say to Maudie: 'We might as well go now.' And then, I don't know if his tuppence ran out, but he got up and he come after me. He said: 'Should I walk you home?' And I said: 'Maudie, I'm now going.'

Poor Maudie. I don't know where she went. She probably had one of the boys walk home with her, but I couldn't care less. Dick never said we'll go courting again. But the next night he was at my house, and that was it. If I hadn't have went up to Mousehold that night, he might have met another girl. I might have met another boy. But I expect that was meant to be.

⊰⊱

It was about this time that something sad happened at home. Brother Frank came back one day and caught Father with a lady of not-very-good-character. I don't know if he actually found them doing anything, but they were upstairs together. Frank was shocked and so he did a silly thing. He told everyone. We were all horrified. My sister Rose was living with us when it happened, 'cause her husband was in the service in Egypt. So she was the one what did all the sorting out. She was a hard-working person, but she did want to dominate everybody. 'We're not staying here,' she said. 'Oh no. We're not living here any more.' If only Father had met a nice lady, we'd have accepted it. But we all loved our mother and we felt that he'd let her down. I was only about seventeen at the time, but I was the one what had to tell him. 'We're all going to leave,' I said when he come home one night. He never asked why. I think he knew. Perhaps if I'd been older, I might have said: 'If you want somebody, find someone nice. But don't associate with that type of woman.'

So, we all left. That was a sad thing for us all. My niece, Edie had been happy with us, but when we left, she had to go. Her half-sister up Pottergate[120] took her in. She lived in a one-room-up and one-room-

[120] A street in the old centre of Norwich

down, so poor Edie had to rough it again. My brother Frank went and lived with my sister Edie for a time. He went into lodgings after that. Poor Frank, it always seemed as though things went wrong with him. Charlie went and lived with Brother Graham. Rose and I went to live in Gresham Road, with my sister, Hilda, and Frank and their four children. She and I shared a bedroom with their daughter, Irene. Irene was about 10 years old then and had a separate little bed. Dick lived close by in Bignold Street. That was really nice and handy for both of us to get together. But poor Hilda, she always had a hard life. Her husband was a clicker, but them were bad times in the boot work. Mostly they only had bread and marge and mashed potato to eat. But Hilda was good. I suppose she took after Mother. She used to make her children clothes on machine. And I think she used to go and scrub a pub out to earn a bit extra. From Hilda's house, I had a good way to work, so I took the bus in the morning and evening. It was tuppence for a return ticket. I couldn't afford fourpence a day on bus fares, so I used to walk there and back at dinner times – half an hour home and half an hour back again. We got off at half past twelve, and started back at two o'clock, so I had half an hour at home.

I was always close to Father, even after we moved out. I used to go back to the old house in Cavalry Street once a week, and keep him clean. I scrubbed his place out. When he was a pensioner, he used to come and meet me from work. And I'd give him a shilling for tobacco. That was eleven pence I think, but I used to give him a shilling. After a time the others were alright with him too, and Edie would have him over for Sunday lunch.

One night Dick came to see me. He was very upset. I said: 'What's the matter with you?' 'My mother's having a baby,' he said. He was very indignant. 'Ah, it's disgusting!' he say. I think he thought his mother and father didn't do things like that. 'You mustn't be like that with your mother,' I said to Dick. 'That can happen.' But it was sad that she was having this baby after she'd already got six and his father was out of work. In the end, it came to nothing. That was little Albert. He had a cord round his neck and they lost him.

Dick's family were very, very poor. They lived in a yard up Magpie Road. It was a two-roomed house. Bare floors. Not much furniture. They had to share the copper and everything. They were all on their uppers.[121] He had a brother and four sisters. The children and the parents all slept in the one bedroom. I think he said his mother had a curtain across. Dick was the eldest, so when he was about fourteen, he went and slept at his grandmother's. He liked going there, but he had to sleep in the loft. He said there was rats running all about and that he used to try and get to sleep quick before they started to run over the top of him.[122]

Dick's father used to sit by the fire with his feet up by the side of the stove. He could never get a job, you see. He was a turn shoemaker

[121] Extremely short of money and resources.

[122] Rats infested many areas of the city. The *Norwich Mercury* for this period features numerous advertisements for rat poisoning and many rat-related stories. In March 1920, there was a report of a court case in which a tenant in Ten Bell Lane was refusing to pay rent till the landlord solved the rat problem. She claimed that there were about 50 rat holes in the house and that the rats had bitten her children and eaten her food. The Court Chairman asked the city's chief sanitary inspector whether the house was fit for habitation and he responded: 'I should say so with the exception of the rats'. On this, the tenant had to agree to pay rent and arrears. Earlier in the year, an account of a City Council meeting recorded: 'Sir Ailwyn Fellowes called the attention of the committee to the fact that the Rat Order came into force on January 1st and therefore anybody who failed to kill his rats was liable to a penalty of £20.'

by trade. That was one what did everything by hand. It was a skilled job, but that went out when the machinery come in. I suppose he was in his 30s or 40s at the time, and he couldn't do no more turn shoemaking ever. I'll give him his due. He did want a job. But he didn't know machinery, and nobody would learn him. Him and thousands of others used to be on the bureau nearly all the time. That meant they didn't get hardly any money. They were really, really on the breadline. His father were on the means test as they used to call it. It was mean an' all. Every little while, they used to give him an eight-week job. He couldn't pick and choose. He had to do what they said. On the roads or whatever. But he used to pray for that to come round, 'cause when he got it, he had a wage, and it gave him an uplift. But eight weeks wasn't long.[123]

Though he was out of work, he'd be smoking the Woodbines. He liked to drink, and he liked his cigarette. He was a rough man, a stern man, and he was very uncultivated. He was always shouting at people. He never said a kind word to Dick and his brother. He'd be behind the door and hit Dick as he come in. He used to make him do the washing up. I never could see why he should have had to do that, being a boy. His mother used to clear the table and Dick would sit there, wanting to go out. 'Father, can I wash up?' he'd say. 'No, not yet,' he said, all grumpy, sitting in his chair. At last he'd say: 'You can wash up now.' When Dick finished, he'd say: 'Can I go out now?' His father said: 'No, it's too late now.'

<hr>

[123] Unemployment, already high, rose further during the years of economic depression in the 1920s and 30s. The Norwich local government had some success in relieving it by undertaking large-scale public works projects; notably the construction of a new City Hall and Eaton and Wensum Parks, slum clearance and the construction of new housing estates.

Dick got his looks from his mother. She was a tiny woman, a pretty little woman. But she'd a hard life. She was a poor little thing when I knew her. She wasn't old really, but she had her hair in wirelesses, and that made her look old. That was when they parted it down the middle, made two braids, and then wrapped one braid round each ear. It was like looking at someone with headphones on. She was afraid of his father. Women were in them days. They didn't stand up to their husbands.

I got on alright with Dick's father, but Dick, with his memories, he hated him. One Saturday night his father was out and his mother got them all bathed. Dick emptied the bath water with her, 'cause it took two to carry it. Then in come his father with a whole gang of people. They weren't drunk, but they'd had a drink, and they bought all this beer back. 'Poor mother she'd only then finished bathing us,' Dick told me. He was sorry for her. It tire you out bathing the children, and she didn't need people in there with all this beer. They didn't have no telly, or wireless, or nothing, but she should have been able to have a sit down. When they went, his mother said something about why d'you bring them all home? He go to hit her. But Dick then jumped up and hit his father. He was only fourteen, but he'd been boxing and he knew how to fight. And it shook the old man. He didn't hit him back. I suppose he was too stunned. And after that he weren't so bad to Dick and his brother. I reckon he thought: 'The kid's strong. He's going to give me one.' And never after that did his father ever do anything like that no more

Dick's mother had arthritis. I felt sorry for the poor old girl. When she did her washing, she had to wring everything out by hand, 'cause she had no mangle. We'd all left father's house by then and so one day

I say to him: 'Can Dick's mother have the wringer, Father?' 'Yes, she can,' he said. But the thing of it was we had to push it all the way. We shoved that wringer all the way along the city streets. I used to do the ironing for her sometimes. The clothes I ironed were worn thin. But people didn't cast things off in those days.

❦

Dick and me kept courting, but he still didn't have any money, 'cause he couldn't get a job. Jimmy, my sister Nelly's husband had got his cards, so it were hard for them an' all. They had two rooms on Elm Hill. One holiday Monday, Nelly asked me and Dick to sleep over at her place. Not that we slept together. We wouldn't even think about it. I slept with Nelly, and Dick slept with Jimmy. The next day, Nelly said: 'What about us going up the river?' 'We're game,' we all say. We didn't have much money, but we had enough to hire a boat. We went up the river and that was lovely. And Jimmy say: 'Have you got a smoke, Dick?' 'No,' he say, 'I'm out of cigarettes.' 'Well, I've got one,' say Jimmy. 'So we'll have half each.' Two grown-up men – one was married and one was eighteen – with only one cigarette between them! And then as Jimmy was getting it out of his cigarette case, he dropped it and it fell through the boards into the bottom of the boat. We had to go a bit further up the river before we could stop and get the boat out of the water. They turned it upside down, and a huge, green frog jumped out. They found the cigarette in the end. After that, we went a little further up the river to a pub. Nelly gave them a shilling each before we went in. She was working at the time. Dick and Jimmy had a beer and Nelly and me had a port and lemon. That was 1/4d in all. They then whisper to us: 'When we ask you if you want another drink, you have to say no.'

Nelly used to have Dick and me and my brother Charlie round there regular to play cards. Dick never had no money. Not like my brother Charlie. He had a good job, and he was a boy what took care of his money. He used to say: 'Look what I've got, Ethel.' And he'd get a handful of pay packets out what he'd never even opened. I don't suppose he meant it, but it broke my heart. When we used to play cards, Charlie had his hand full of florins and half crowns. And Dick would get about five pennies out. That was all what he had, and perhaps I gave him thruppence of that. They used to play Knockback.[124] And Charlie always used to win. One night, Charlie say to me: 'I'm going to get engaged next weekend.' And I say: 'Ooh, are you?' Dick was there, so I didn't say nothing else, but I was ever so sad. I knew no way Dick could afford to give me a ring. He didn't have nothing for himself. When Charlie got the ring, Maude, his fiancée shew me, 'cause she used to come round with him sometimes. I said: 'Oh lovely for you.' But after she'd gone, I bursted out crying. Charlie say: 'What you crying for?' I say: 'I'll never have an engagement ring.' He then put his arm round me and sang: 'Some day there'll be a silver lining. The clouds will soon roll by.'

The next week when we went to my sister Nelly's, Dick say: 'I'm not going to play cards tonight. I'm going over to the Corn Hall.' That's where they done the boxing contests. The one that won got twenty-five shillings, but you used to have to fight whoever came up. They didn't weigh-in at that time, so it could be that the young man you were fighting was a stone more than you. And some of them what come up from the country were big burly boys. Dick was a real boxer,

124 A card game with rules much the same as Whist.

but he wasn't very big.   He rang the bell when he came back, and I opened the door. 'Look, I've twenty-five shillings,' he say. 'I'll save some for a ring, and we'll have a night out properly.'

Dick

Normally on a night out we used to have to go in the five-penny seats in the cinema. We didn't go in pubs. But on that special night out, when we were 'flush', he took me in the 1/3d seats, which were posh. We booked 'em, so we could go in and the lady would show us our seats. We sat in these lovely seats and he put a small box of chocolates on my lap. I suppose they were Caley's about sixpence a quarter of a pound. And when we went out, we had a 'two and a one' – a tuppenny bit of fish, and a pennorth of chips, where in the normal way we just had a pennorth of chips or a quarter of Licorice Allsorts. But this night we had fish *and* chips, which was wonderful. We felt like we were millionaires. Of course, Dick had to keep most of the money for the ring, so he dursen't spend too much. But it was a special night, and we felt special, for a change.

The following week he said: 'I'm going in again.' He done the same, and he won again. And the third week he done it, and he got the twenty-five shillings again. Then he went the fourth week. I was at my sister's on Elm Hill. She had a lovely house with a glass front door. When we heard the door knock, I said: 'Oh that's Dick.' There was a light from outside, and I could see his face through the glass. I nearly died. 'Oh no,' I said. His poor eyes were bunged up, his mouth was bleeding, and his nose was spread across. I opened the door and I said: 'Oh, whatever have they done to you?' He say: 'I didn't win. I only drawed. The bloke was a big country boy, two stone more than me and he didn't box, he fought.' I loved him and kissed his poor face, and cried. 'You in't going to fight no more... no more, I say. I never did hear what his mother said about it. She must have been frantic, and hated me for that, 'cause she knew he was wanting the money to buy a ring. It was wonderful having the money he won, and we did get enough for the ring. But I never let him box no more.

Elm Hill, where Nelly and Jimmy lived

18. The Engagement and the Wedding

The next Saturday we tripped up to Dipple's on Swan Lane. We looked in the window and then we went in and saw this lovely ring. It was like a daisy, a diamond in the middle and little ones round it like petals. Then there were two more diamonds, one on each side. It was gorgeous, and it cost three guineas. I come out of that shop as though I was ten feet tall. Dick was pleased. My sisters were pleased. We were all happy. He never asked my father's permission to get engaged, because I weren't living at home then, but we went over to Dick's to tell his mother. 'Do you like my ring?' I say. 'It's all right, but he should have had a new suit,' she said. My big bubble burst. All the excitement had gone. Oh, she had a sharp little tongue. Of course, she was right in a way. He should have had a new suit. But I suppose he loved me and he wanted to buy this ring.

When Dick was out of work, he used to go every day to every factory in Norwich. He used to leave home before eight with his apron and his tools. And everywhere he went, he had to walk, 'cause his mother had made him sell his bike when he finished his bureau money. Poor Dick. He was right up the Drayton Road and all the factories were in the city. Once or twice I treated him to have his boots mended, 'cause I was better off than he was, but the rest of the time he had cardboard on the soles of his feet. He used to say to me: 'I keep going down to the Co-op, 'cause if you get a job at the Co-op Boot and Shoe Operatives, it's a job for life.' The man what used to set them on there was a lovely man, and he really liked Dick. He used to say: 'No boy, I haven't got nothing for you today, but I assure you, when we do get something you'll be in, cause you're so willing and you come every day.'

One day when I was over at my sister Hilda's, Dick come over for the evening. All we had for dinner was bread and butter and a potato, 'cause my brother-in-law were out of work and they didn't have nothing else. We were playing a game of cards, when one of Dick's sisters ran over. 'Dicky,' she say 'there's a man over the road what want to speak to you.' Dick had his coat on the back of a chair, and he just grabbed it and ran. That was to say that he could start at the Co-op, but only temporary, 'cause someone was away sick. In the end, they kept him, 'cause he was good on machines. So as soon as he got this regular job, he bought a bike to get to work.

But then, soon after he'd got the job, he said to me: 'I don't know what we're going to do. I've got to keep house now.' Five children and a mother and father, and Dick had to keep them all, because he was earning money. He had to give his mother everything what he was earning. One of his sisters was working by then, but she used to sleep at someone else's, so she could say she wasn't living at home. That was underhanded really, and what a sad thing that she had to do it. 'We can't go on like this,' I said to Dick. We should be going out and enjoying ourselves, but we can't. The best thing we can do is get married, because really we'll never get anywhere if you got to keep your family.' You see, as soon as Dick got out of the house, they'd give his father the money again. So we told his mother and father that we were going to get married. I don't think his mother liked it much.

I went over to see Father, and I said: 'Can we have your front room and the big bedroom?' They were two lovely rooms, and he didn't need the whole house to himself. Father said yes, and so Charlie come and done the front room all out. He was very good at that sort of thing, and he done it all for nothing. In them days, you wouldn't even think about asking someone to do you a job and giving them money 'cause nobody had any. So we had it all done out lovely. A picture rail, linoleum and a rug I bought. And we had all new furniture. Lovely stuff. I got the best of everything. A beautiful walnut bedroom suite, a lovely dining room table, four dining room chairs and two lovely fireside chairs. Cowhide, they were. Of course, we didn't have no money, so we had to get it on the mace.[125] Five shillings down and so much a week. I'd already been buying little things here and little things there. So by then, I had everything to put in the home with regards to utensils and little vases. At that time of day, people didn't buy you much when you got married. They'd buy you perhaps a Duchess set[126] or two tea towels or a towel, but that was it.

⊰⊱

I always wanted to be married in white, but I didn't have the money to buy a wedding dress. My sister-in-law, Charlie's wife, she had a lovely satin gown, all done beautifully, and a lovely veil. And she lent me them. I bought a sixpenny pair of white cashmere gloves to go with the dress, and a pair of velvet white shoes. They were from Baxter's and Webster's, where I was working at the time. You could get samples if you worked there, so when these come along I thought: 'I'll have them.' The samples were size 4 only. Luckily that was my size. They were a pound. And then I had a lovely bouquet. Mrs Worthingham up

---

[125] On hire purchase or a credit arrangement.

[126] A set of three dressing-table mats.

Exchange Street done it. She used to make beautiful flower tributes. Big chrysanthemums coming down with loads of green. That was really the best thing I had. Dick had a new suit, 'cause he was then working. I think that was on hire purchase. He looked lovely with his white shirt and lovely tie. We got married on Boxing Day. I remember getting up early and playing all Christmas carols on the gramophone. You know the old ones with a horn. Whether Hilda, borrowed it, I don't know. I can't remember it being there all the time. And I thought when I got up: 'Oh I'm going to marry my lovely Dick. We're going to sleep together. We're going to live together.'

There was snow about. Dick's mother and father and his brother and four sisters were there, but not all of my family came. In them days, everyone went to funerals. Yes, they would definitely go to a funeral, 'cause that was to pay their last respects. Wherever they lived, they'd get there somehow. But they'd only go to a wedding if they lived near. There was just Nelly, Frank, Rose, and Hilda and her husband. Dick and his best man and most of 'em walked to St Luke's Church. The rest got a bus. Of course, you didn't walk through the street with a white veil and white shoes, so Father and me had a taxi. 'You don't have to be there on time,' Father say. 'You have to make him wait.' That's why we were a long time getting to the church. I think they were all getting a bit worried. Father give me away, and my sister Nelly was my matron of honour. She had a nice blue dress on. She took the bouquet when I had to make the vows. After the wedding, Dick and I got in the taxi and went to Baldry's in Magdalen Street and had a photo taken. We just went in, had our photo taken and come out and took a taxi home. I don't know why we didn't have Nelly on.

Our wedding

We had the party at Dick's mother's house, but she didn't buy nothing. She didn't have no money. And neither did my father. His pension was only ten shillings a week, and he'd never saved. (I can remember Mother once telling me why. She said that he had a brother what was in the navy and one time when he was home, he stole all father's money when he went back to sea. That was a good bit of money what he'd saved, and it did something to Father. He never forgave his brother, and he never saved up any more after that.) So I was the one what paid for the wedding. I had to borrow five shillings off Mr Carver. We did it on a shoestring. I got two or three tins of salmon and crab. And we had some salad and sausage rolls what my sisters made. And Jimmy, Nelly's husband, brought some cockles and whelks from his father's market stall. He couldn't come to the wedding, 'cause he was working. But as soon as the stall closed and he could get away, he come to Dick's mother's. Then we had buns, jelly and custard and a tin of pineapple and a tin of pears. I got a Christmas cake. It wasn't very dear. Just a little round white cake. I took the snowman off, and went and got a little wedding thing to put on instead. It was a lovely spread what we had. We had a gallon pewter thing with a big round cork that was full of ale. And a few stouts for the wives. And we sang, like we always used to, taking turns around the room. We had a lovely turn out. What a cheap wedding, but what a lovely wedding.

When it got to twelve o'clock, I went to the bedroom to get all my wedding attire off. Dick's mother was with me. We were talking and Dick came into the room. I just had my petticoat on, so I go to cover myself up, and she say: 'Oh, you mustn't be like that. He's your husband now.' We had to walk back to Cavalry Street. We'd moved in with Father, so he walked home with us. Fancy having to walk home on your wedding night, all that way from Drayton Road to Mousehold Street, about three quarters of an hour. We didn't get to bed till late. And then Dick had to go to go to work at 7 o'clock the next morning. The blokes laughed at him, 'cause it was his first night. He always used to say: 'Oh Ethel, I'd have give anything if we could have had a honeymoon. To think, we could have went away and laid in bed in the morning. He weren't thinking nothing nasty. It was all lovely love.

We were both young, him being twenty-one years old and me twenty. We didn't have much money and we had to get our home on hire purchase, but we were really, really in love. Sometimes we'd wake up about two in the morning and he'd say to me: 'Ethel, are you hungry?' And we used to get up and fry bacon and have bacon sandwiches. They were delicious. We'd sit up in bed eating them, laughing and joking. A few years after that, the war came. But that's another story.

Hilda's wedding during the Great War

Mother's child-bearing years were from 1888 until 1914, so that Albert, her first child, was 26 when Ethel was born.

Ethel's Family

Father: Albert Ernest Edwards
Birth: 18 November 1870, Heigham, Norwich
Death: December 1943, Norwich
Married   24 May 1890, Norwich

Mother: Eleanor Susannah Chaplin
Birth: 21 July 1870, Norwich
Death: 21 October 1931, Norwich

Children: Albert (1888-1936)

Clara (1890-1976)

Frederic Samuel (1892-1942)

Graham (1895-1963)

Robert (1896-1897)

Hilda Florence (1897-1976)

George (1898-1899)

Walter (1899-1963)

Samuel (1900-1959)

Edith Maud (1901-1995)

William (1904-1984)

Rose Gertrude (1906-1970)

Frank (1907-1908)

Frank (1909-1970)

Eleanor (1910-1997)

Charles Arthur (1913-1975)

Ethel Eva (1914-)

Picture credits

The photographs on pages 6, 98, 106, 111, 144, 146, 161, 173, 174, 197, 203, 206 and on the front and back cover are in the possession of the author.

The following photographs have kindly been supplied by Norfolk County Council Library and Information Service from the Picture Norfolk Archive:

p.18	NP00001778
p.48	NP00013536
p.59	NP00002353
p.63	*NP00013554
p.66	*NP00002004
p.86 (top)	*NP00013297
p.86 (bottom)	NP00012566
p.90 (top left)	NP00001507
p.90 (top right)	NP00001277
p.90 (bottom left)	#NP00001336
p.90 (bottom right)	*NP00013504
p.112	*NP00013082
p.113	NP00001518
p. 116 (top)	NP00001357
p.116 (bottom)	*NP00013126
p.117	NP00007455
p.120	NP00014583
p.121	NP00009497
p.131	NP00001632
p.133	NP00008446
p.156	NP00014531
p.158	NP00003957

(by kind permission of A.E.Coe and Son, Castle Meadow, Norwich)

p.164	NP00002261
p.198	NP00001483

★ Photographer George Swain
 # Photographer W. Buston